VIGNETTES

T0358079

Vignettes

Series Editors: Tony Hughes-d'Aeth and Sarah Collins

The Vignettes Series from UWAP is aimed at sharing the knowledges that are emerging in the contemporary university and that consider the complexities of modern life. Each book provides an image, or a vignette, of a particular phenomenon and how this is being thought through by intellectual practitioners in today's academy.

Books in This Series

- *Netflicks: Conceptual Television in the Streaming Era* by Tony Hughes-d'Aeth
- *The Moment of the Essay* by Daniel Juckes (forthcoming)
- *Saving Heritage Breeds: a Love Story* by Catie Gressier (forthcoming)
- *Artificial Life* by Oron Catts, Sarah Collins, Elizabeth Stephens and Ionat Zurr (forthcoming)
- *Australiana* by Graham Akhurst and Penni Russon (forthcoming)

VIGNETTES

Netflicks
Conceptual Television in the Streaming Era

TONY HUGHES-D'AETH

First published in 2024 by
UWA Publishing
Crawley, Western Australia 6009
www.uwap.uwa.edu.au

UWAP is an imprint of UWA Publishing
a division of The University of Western Australia

UWA Publishing acknowledges we are situated on Noongar land, and that
Noongar people remain the spiritual and cultural custodians of their land,
and continue to practice their values, languages, beliefs and knowledge.
We pay our respects to the traditional owners of the lands on which we
live and work across Western Australia and Australia.

ISBN: 978-1-76080-272-1

A catalogue record for this
book is available from the
National Library of Australia

Cover design by Mika Tabata
Typeset in 11 point Garamond by Lasertype
Printed by McPherson's Printing Group

 uwapublishing

MIX
Paper | Supporting
responsible forestry
FSC® C001695

Contents

Introduction

Conceptual Television in the Streaming Era

It seemed to happen overnight. Not long ago, we were all watching television, and now we are watching something else. The television station has been replaced by the streaming service. Well, not quite replaced, since we still have television, but somehow our television screens are not quite what they were. This book is about televisual drama in the streaming age, and it considers some of the continuities that contemporary streamed shows have to other narrative forms – most notably, classic television and classic Hollywood – as well as elements that seem either genuinely novel or, at the least, newly urgent. One of the distinctive elements of televisual drama in the streaming era is its recourse to concept. Certainly, there are dozens of programs that seem very much to follow earlier genres, but there is also an important subset of shows that seem to be concerned with thinking through concepts that form the basis of social existence. It is these programs that I am calling 'conceptual television'.

In this book, I consider four main concepts: dystopia, amnesia, repetition and dissociation. Key to my exposition of these concepts is the contention that what conceptual television makes visible at the level of its concept is the unconscious. The concepts considered in this book all attempt to represent unconscious processes. And, at the same time, these unconscious processes are also linked to social imperatives. Dystopia manifests the most fundamental fears about social life, yet it also introduces a domain that permits the fulfilment of hidden wishes. Amnesia is the conceptual trope that dramatises the action of repression, but it is also places a distinct value on what is repressed, insisting that it is not separable from human life. Shows based on repetition, such as those involving a time loop, literalise the compulsion to repeat, but inside this apparently futile cycle is the fundamental structure of education. The splitting of worlds, which I have called dissociation, creates the narrative conditions for social critique, but also alludes to a foundational difference that seems to exist *within* us. By granting the unconscious this determinative dimension (that is, the status of a founding concept), what conceptual television offers is a positivisation of the excluded elements of social reality.

A key characteristic of television is its ephemerality. I have chosen examples of these concepts from the particular time in which I have written this book. It is possible you have seen the shows I discuss, or that you are aware of them. It is equally possible that you have not watched nor even heard of them. Don't despair! I provide enough detail that you can follow the discussion even if you have not watched the shows. More importantly, what I try to do is to take the shows up to a level of generality so that my assertions can be understood in relation to other shows of the kind I discuss. For instance, my analysis of *The Walking Dead* (2010–) in Chapter One will apply, with only minor adjustments, to most zombie narratives, or indeed most films and shows that involve an apocalyptic scenario. I offer particular examples not to necessarily fix a canon of important works – though, hopefully, I have selected shows and films of some cultural significance – but to show how concepts are presented within the shows. It is only by examining the detail of a show that we can see the narrative dynamics and the formal movements of these screen texts. The shows used as examples in this book should allow you to reason both back to earlier shows and forward to new ones.

A New Temporality

One of the ways in which we know we are entering new territory is that television has begun to appear as a historical moment. That is, it appears on our screens as something we used to do. In the first episode of the Marvel superhero show, *WandaVision* (2021), we find ourselves watching what looks like a comedy from the early days of television. There is the basic *mise-en-scène* of TV sitcom, namely the living room that stands as an expression of the home and the nuclear family. The screen is black and white, and the aspect ratio is the squarish 4:3 of classic TV, rather than the more elongated rectangle 16:9 of current shows. The superhero characters Wanda and Vision have somehow dropped out of the Marvel Cinematic Universe, where they fight villains as part of the Avengers superhero ensemble, and into the quaint banality of 1950s TV sitcoms like *I Love Lucy* (1951–57) and *The Honeymooners* (1955–56).

The action is punctuated by the synchronised cackle of canned laughter as the two superheroes act out the rituals and incidental absurdities of 1950s gender roles. In subsequent episodes, the show's *mise-en-scène* modulates into iconic sitcoms from each ensuing decade, such as *Bewitched* (1964–72), *The Brady Bunch* (1969–74), *Full House* (1987–95), *Malcolm in the Middle* (2000–06), *Friends* (1994–2004) and *Modern Family* (2009–20). In this way, *WandaVision* seems to give a literal expression to Marshall McLuhan's dictum that the content of a medium is always another medium. According to this line of thought, we know we are in a new medium because we can see an older medium. In *WandaVision*, the boxy 4:3 aspect ratio is not experienced as the structuring limit of the visible – that is, the edge of the screen, indeed the edge of the mediated world – but as a stylisation.

But what, really, has changed? Surely, we have just moved from one mode of delivery to another. Indeed, as TV streaming services have proliferated, I sometimes betray my age by asking people what 'channel' a particular show is on. In other words, I am perceiving Netflix, Disney+, HBO and so on as equivalent to the network channels of the broadcast

Wandavision courtesy of Alamy.

NETFLICKS

era. Perhaps the most significant difference between broadcast television (including cable and satellite television) and streaming services is their respective relationships to time.

Broadcast television, like radio, is strictly timetabled. The content is not ascribed willy-nilly to the hours of the day, but carefully follows the rhythms of social life, such that we have morning, daytime, evening and late-night television. Likewise, there are noticeable differences between weekday and weekend television. Television also adopted the practice of having 'seasons' and summer breaks, and so would also mimic the calendar year. In all of these ways, television was intimately bound to social time. Furthermore, as we became more connected to television, it was clear that, in some ways, television was not just following social time but helping to constitute it, with the evening news, for instance, signalling the end of the working day.

All of this disappears in the world of streamed content. The content is not provided at specific times, but sits there as a kind of permanent archive that can be accessed on demand. The implications flowing from this shift are quite profound. In the first instance, we see a partition at the level of content. The fictional dimension of television (dramas, comedies, movies) that used to sit inside the framework of socialised television time were found to be more attractively situated in the on-demand digital archive that was offered by Netflix and its imitators.

Again, this, in itself, might not seem too earth shattering. Indeed, the process had, to a large extent, been prefigured by the emergence of DVD boxsets. This had already started to significantly change viewing habits, as viewers could purchase whole series and watch them, if they had the desire and the stamina, in a single sitting. In other words, binge-watching preceded the emergence of streaming services. There was also, prior to the emergence of on-demand streaming, a division that emerged between cheap-and-cheerful broadcast shows like *Big Bang Theory* (2007–19) and 'prestige' television programs like *The Sopranos* (1999–2007), *Six Feet Under* (2001–05) and *The Wire* (2002–08) being produced by the American cable channel HBO. In this context, the move to make these kinds of programs, along with a back catalogue of movies, available online rather than via the hard format of DVD and Blu-ray, seems simply an evolution that is based on technological convenience.

What was novel about the emergence of Netflix was that series were, for the first time, released in full and online. Its seminal dramas from this moment, *House of Cards* (2013–18) and *Orange is the New Black* (2013–19), were released as full seasons. This felt qualitatively different to a DVD boxset because, in the case of the boxset, the shows had first aired on their respective television channels and then, so it seemed, were collected up and re-issued to those who wanted their own copy. Again, this seemingly small change had quite a profound effect.

The Digital Public Sphere

In the first instance, what streamed content announced was that the online world was a place of primary cultural emergence. Cultural narratives were now issuing from cyberspace, which was where they were born and where they lived and where, presumably, they must also die. Until this moment, there was still, by and large, a sense that the internet was a private, person-to-person domain and that public culture was still more properly located in traditional media: newspapers, radio, cinema and, most important of all, television. Television was the medium of daily life *par excellence*. These are large claims, to be sure, and the process is more complex, with many cross-currents and counter-examples. Yet, if one is looking for a moment of sentience, a certain critical inflexion point or singularity in which the public sphere shifted decisively from a nodal broadcast paradigm to that of internet mediation, then the year 2013 in which Netflix began 'dropping' full seasons of its shows is a good candidate.

Releasing a television program in full and online instigated a new dispensation that can be seen in how it suddenly made all the usual terminology seem antiquated. A television 'program' was no longer a program, because in an on-demand environment it is not programmed. Nor is it really a 'show' since it is not shown; it is now simply watched. We still speak of a 'season' to refer to a show's narrative arc, but really, this term loses its meaning when it is no longer part of the calendrical time that broadcast television subsisted in and helped to constitute. The term 'episode' is still valid, but it has lost the determining imperatives that once gave the television episode its shape and size. An episode no longer needs to fit 30- or 60-minute slots, nor be scripted to accommodate regular ad breaks. In fact, there is no longer any necessity for the shows to be of a fixed duration, and modern streamed drama episodes now vary in length.

Even so, all of these effects might still be counted as fairly minor adjustments to what is still a fairly similar product. The dramatic content that streaming services create are still recognisably the genres that emerged in the broadcast era: soap operas, documentaries, situation comedies, police procedurals, Westerns, science fiction serials, political thrillers, period drama and so on. So again, what, if anything, has really changed?

Conceptual Television

This is the question that this short book, in its analysis of conceptual television, seeks in part to answer. The argument I present here is that we do have an overt continuity of form in that contemporary streamed drama is indeed the formal heir to practices of mediated dramaturgy that were formalised decisively with the emergence of classical Hollywood in the 1910s. While Hollywood obviously evolved significantly in the 100 years since the crystallisation of its classical style – most notably with the introduction of synchronised sound in the late 1920s and colour film stock in the 1940s – its basic formal practices have been retained and constitute the invisible assumptions of all screened drama.

But, in this book, I also suggest that the translocation of screen drama into the digital domain – not just as a method of delivery, but as the understood habitat of its being – represents a decisive step whose consequences are yet to fully materialise, but are erupting symptomatically through various features of contemporary televisual drama. This argument is one that proceeds by induction insofar as I am reasoning back from the stylistic symptoms of contemporary streamed drama to posit digital streaming as a material cause. I start with a specific subset of television drama that I am calling conceptual television, and which refers to shows that are based on an overt conceptual premise.

In particular, I consider four concepts that have recurred with some frequency already in the relatively short history of streamed television. In each case, examples of the concept can be traced to before streaming, so my claim is not that they emerge for the first time in this era, but rather, they take on a particular inflexion today. The opening chapter explores the prolific genre known as dystopia. This genre contains some of the most popular shows in the streaming era, including *The Walking Dead*, *The Handmaid's Tale* (2017–) and *Squid Game* (2021), and the chapter discusses each of these programs. Within the terms of this book, I am treating dystopia as a 'concept' insofar as it is based on a world-determining premise. In dystopia, the premise is that the old world has disappeared, and a new and worse world has emerged in its place. Intriguingly, this new 'dystopian' world inevitably actualises qualities that were implicit in the old world and, in this respect, the dystopian world reveals the unconscious coordinates of the world that has gone. In this chapter, I suggest that the distinction between utopia and dystopia is not as useful as is usually imagined and, in fact, it is best to think of dystopia as a form of utopia insofar as it enacts key wishes, fantasies and compensations. I also suggest that dystopia has proliferated because of its capacity to challenge 'capitalist realism', which is a term used to describe the way that capitalism strictly delimits the parameters of what is realistic.

The second concept I consider is amnesia. The amnesia plot is a familiar device in twentieth-century cinema, although it is interesting that there are not many amnesiacs in literature from the nineteenth century or earlier. The second chapter examines the recurrence of amnesia in contemporary streamed television, and suggests how it galvanises particular forms of doubt that now attach to memory. Drawing particularly on the examples of

I May Destroy You (2020) and *Homecoming* (2018–20), the chapter suggests that there has been an unconscious absorption of the idea of computer memory (data storage) into the assumed operation of human memory.

In the third chapter, I focus on the particular form of repetition that finds itself expressed in the time loop stories of contemporary television. In these shows, the hero of the story finds themselves trapped in a particular day of their life that endlessly repeats. Again, the device of the time loop predates streamed television, notably in the influential comedy film *Groundhog Day* (1993). But the reappearance of this concept in today's streamed dramas, such as in *Russian Doll* (2019–22) and *The Rehearsal* (2022), helps bring out the basic features of the time loop in narrative and subjective terms. In short, the time loop functions as a contemporary form of the *bildungsroman*, which now takes place under the sign of repetition. The suggestion is that, today, childhood and adolescence are no longer able to fulfil their function of inducing maturation. The time loop comes in to rescue those trapped in adult infantilism by forcing them to relive a single day endlessly until they have learned their lesson.

In the fourth chapter, there is also a kind of repetition, though not in the form of an endlessly repeated day, but rather in the reduplication of the world. I have characterised the concept in which a show is populated by parallel worlds as one of 'dissociation' because there is always some irreducible difference that the doubling helps expose. In this way, the parallel-world story involves the dissociation of one world – and its key characters – from their counterparts in their other world. I offer *Counterpart* (2017–19) as an example of this concept. In this show, a scientific experiment in Cold War Berlin inadvertently opens a portal from one universe to another that is initially identical. But as time passes, the worlds drift apart and become hostile to one another. Another show that exemplifies dissociation is *Severance* (2022–), in which a medical procedure allows a person to fully 'sever' their work self from their private self. The 'severed' worker goes in each day, passes through a special elevator, and immediately forgets the entirety of their life 'outside'. At the end of the day, they pass back through the elevator and forget everything that occurred while in the office.

In each of these chapters, I advance the idea that conceptual television has emerged as a very particular challenge to the determinations of the world that we do, in fact, inhabit. Conceptual television exposes the limitations of realism and the crucial dimensions of human life that are missed in the common-sense account of reality. And yet, the conceptual programs included in this book expose a dimension of ourselves that we somehow already know but cannot countenance because it is incompatible with the precepts of our social realism. What is strange about conceptual television is that it *does* make sense. Despite the seemingly outlandish premises – sudden and specific amnesias, endlessly recurring time loops, portals to parallel universes, hordes of zombies roaming the earth – as audiences, we are immediately able to relate to what takes place. In fact, while what takes place should be strange or mind-blowing, instead, it all feels oddly familiar.

Chapter One

Dystopia

Dystopia has become a fixture of contemporary fiction, film and television. The paradigm was established in the late nineteenth century with H.G. Wells' *The Time Machine* (1895) and includes key works, such as Aldous Huxley's *Brave New World* (1932), George Orwell's *Nineteen Eighty-Four* (1949) and Margaret Atwood's *The Handmaid's Tale* (1985). Dystopian stories are set in the future, often the near future, or sometimes an alternative present. They typically depict a society that has either fallen into disrepair following some disaster, or where the instrumental aims of techno-modernity have reached a hideous consummation. In both cases, what is being imagined is an alternative to what Mark Fisher called 'capitalist realism'.

Fisher uses the term 'capitalist realism' to suggest that any attempt to suggest an alternative to market-driven wealth concentration is considered 'unrealistic'. In other words, the capitalist order forecloses alternatives, not through brute force, but by consigning them to the realm of fantasy. By proffering the market as a hallowed encryption of social desire, capitalist societies delimit the boundaries of what is real and rational (socially desired) and what is unreal and irrational. Dystopian fiction can be regarded as a means to think through this impasse, drawing on the alibi of fictionality to offer up alternatives to the status quo that are permitted to escape the rules of the real world.

It is interesting that the bleak possibilities of dystopia, rather than rosy visions of utopia, have proved far more fertile for thinking through the conditions of capitalist realism. The swerve to dystopia, rather than utopia, seems to be the price paid to have fictions that contest reality. In other words, dystopias want to challenge capitalism's privileged relationship to realism, knowing that anything too openly utopian would immediately be patronised as nice, but unrealistic. In capitalist societies, it is the 'invisible hand' of the market that constitutes the final law. The market is understood as a kind of vote, wherein a multitude of micro-transactions aggregate to express a resultant (a share-price, for example) that glows with the aura once reserved for papal edicts.

The overwhelming success of capitalism in colonising human communities in the past 200 years has certainly lent a strong sense of inevitability to its dispensations of value, such that it has indeed become very difficult to see how it can end except through some cataclysm. Thus, dystopian fictions will often rely on some radical emergence – a horrifying virus, the return of the living dead, the eruption of nuclear war, the arrival of hostile aliens from outer space – as the condition for social alternatives to capitalism. Yet, in many ways, the distinction between dystopian and utopian fiction is illusory, and it is better to think, even though it is a little counter-intuitive, of dystopian fiction as the current modality of utopian fiction.

The Walking Dead

One of the most successful shows of the streaming era is the zombie drama, *The Walking Dead* (2010–), currently in its eleventh season and having spawned two spin-off series. In many ways, the show is a fairly standard zombie story. The zombies spontaneously erupt across the world and relentlessly destroy every institution of organised life. Cities are now desolate wastelands, freeways no longer thrum with cars and trucks, instead standing empty except for occasional burnt-out wreck. Advanced capitalism, which once seemed utterly impervious to challenge, and whose reach seemed to encompass every corner of the planet, is now in ruins, joining all other defunct human empires that imagined they would exist for all time. What the dystopian world induces is a form of dramatic irony. It imagines a point where capitalist realism loses its totalising hold on social reality and becomes an extravagant folly, a vain overreach by humans seduced by their own grandiose pretensions.

What emerges in the wake of capitalism's collapse in *The Walking Dead* is also quite typical of the genre. A small band of survivors, who have somehow escaped the generalised collapse, are thrown together by circumstance. Beginning in a state of mutual mistrust, they nevertheless forge social bonds based on the need to pool resources and survive in the face of the constant menace of the zombies that are seeking to consume them. One of the intriguing features of the zombie genre is that zombies, like vampires, do not kill humans so much as convert them. A zombie, uncouth and inarticulate, relentlessly searches out humans and turns them also into zombies. In this respect, the zombies can be seen as obscene avatars of capitalism itself, which mindlessly roams the earth to find 'new markets', folding more and more people into its voracious system.

But back among the survivors, what takes place is a revitalisation of their social selves. Prior to the zombie apocalypse, these people lived ordinary lives, working as schoolteachers or electricians, police officers or nurses, preoccupied with their iPhones and the empty trivialities of late capitalist existence. After the apocalypse, they become lean and hungry hunter-gatherers, travelling the newly rewilded land in close-knit bands, hunting deer with crossbows and sitting around the campfire each night.

This is how dystopian fictions will often render a utopian political possibility. The men become more 'manly', the women more 'womanly', and empty social niceties are exchanged for a gruff solidarity, a kind of honour among

The Walking Dead courtesy of Alamy.

thieves. Human relations are revitalised and values brought back from their spectral circulation in capitalist exchange, to once again find some firm anchoring in use. In Marxist terms, both things and people (via their alienated labour) revert from their exchange value to their use value. The zombie narrative is thus the condition of a utopian vision of social life rescued from its relentless atomisation through the invisible hand of the market, and re-grounded in real relations and the common good.

The other reason that utopia now takes place under the sign of dystopia is that dystopian fiction insists on social antagonism. The success of capitalist realism partly depends in its offering a solution to social antagonism. Because the invisible hand of the market is making the decisions, it is possible to evade responsibility for social inequality, or indeed intimate that inequality reflects a just distribution of social wealth, with the winners having earned their abundant share and the losers getting their just desserts. Politicians can shrug their shoulders and, with some justification, say that they are themselves slaves to economic reality. Social antagonism is thus neutralised by a broad acceptance that markets are unbiased arbiters of value.

In the face of this virtualisation of social difference by the market, the dystopian text brings back social antagonism, which besets its groups of survivors in different ways. In *The Walking Dead*, at least in the early seasons, we flash back to each character's life before the end of the world. It turns out they were not all saints, and that the contradictions and crimes of their former lives somehow also 'survive' to be acted out on this new and metaphysically sparer stage. Love triangles that existed in the prelapsarian world re-emerge in the zombie-addled present, but this time get worked out authentically, because the characters have had the veil of illusion stripped away. In this way, social antagonism (envy, inequality, resentment, hatred, futility) is given its proper dignity and weight by the presence of the zombies. The zombies are, thus, in their silent, menacing omnipresence at the fringes of the social world of the survivors, the figuration of social antagonism. The utopian dimension of dystopian fiction consists, a little paradoxically, in rendering social antagonism – smuggled out of sight by the market's invisible hand – visible as a fact of social life.

The Handmaid's Tale

Another wildly successful dystopian streamed series is *The Handmaid's Tale* (2017–). This show also introduces a radical rupture in capitalist realism. This time, rather than a complete collapse of the social world, the premise is that the United States is now ruled by religious fundamentalists, and liberal democracy has been replaced by an authoritarian theocracy that calls itself 'Gilead'. The background to this seismic shift in political organisation is a sudden and nearly complete collapse in female fertility. The very few women who can still bear children are identified by the regime and forcibly assigned to the governing elites to provide them with children and heirs. The society is built along strictly patriarchal lines, but in other ways, the world largely seems to resemble a wealthy suburb in capitalist America. The rich still live in large suburban homes and in nuclear families. The main change is that social inequality has been formalised through the existence of female slaves.

Of course, servants are not uncommon in America and other first-world countries, and are a standard feature of wealthy households in the cities of Asia, Africa and Latin America. But what has changed in *The Handmaiden's Tale* is that the pretence of capitalist exchange has been dropped and the female servants are now openly enslaved with no payment and no ability to leave. They are subject to corporal punishment and the petty tyrannies of their lords and ladies. This system of slavery is moralised in the language of sin, so the enslaved women are told they are serving a penance for their sinful actions (adultery, divorce, single motherhood, lesbian sexual orientation), which are thought to undermine the institution of marriage in this patriarchal order. The slavery thus operates as both a source of free domestic labour and a system for controlling and dominating women.

The obscene core of *The Handmaid's Tale*, its primal scene, is what is known reverentially as 'The Ceremony'. Among the servants are the 'handmaids', women who have remained fertile in the face of its widespread decline. In 'The Ceremony', the handmaid is placed in the lap of the

The Handmaid's Tale courtesy of Alamy.

wife while the commander has sex with them. All privacy is stripped from the sexual act and it becomes a semi-public impregnation exercise. But, interestingly, the sexual act is not utterly instrumentalised in *The Handmaid's Tale*. In the dystopian universe of Huxley's *Brave New World*, for example, reproduction takes place entirely *ex utero,* with humans conceived in test tubes and gestated artificially. In *The Handmaid's Tale*, the sexual act retains a certain obscene formality, situated as an ecclesiastical ritual (ceremony) and maintaining its status as a sacrament. There is also a sacrificial dimension, although it is a little ambiguous just what is being sacrificed and on which altar. The participants all maintain a grim solemnity in which subjective enjoyment seems to have been excluded or made taboo. While it is certainly rape in the modern sense, since the handmaids are forced to have sex with the commanders, it is worth remembering that marital rape is not subject to legal sanction in many countries, and even in Western countries is a relatively recent crime, in many cases only criminalised as recently as the 1980s and 1990s.

Master and slave

The traumatic component of The Ceremony derives from its fundamentally ambiguous status in the society of Gilead. In it, the handmaid is simultaneously the abject site of society's sexual violence and the solitary source of its future. Offred, the heroine of the series, acts out this traumatic ambiguity and her suffering constitutes the main dramatic armature of the series. As noted, the sexual act, in which Offred is sandwiched between Commander Waterford and his wife Serena Joy, is in many ways the lingering image of the entire program. Yet, how do we interpret this moment?

The general view is that the show peels back an underlying masculine impulse to control women, and that the dystopian scenario alludes to a multitude of horrific instances of sexual violence and gendered denigration occurring in the real world. It references the restriction of the rights of women in Islamic fundamentalist societies, but also the rise of Christian fundamentalism in America and its obsession with women's reproduction. Indeed, the handmaid is understood to be emblematic of female oppression constellated around the moment of reproduction. In protesting the overturning of the *Roe v Wade* decision by the Supreme Court of the United States in 2022, women gathered in various US cities dressed in handmaid costumes. Without doubt, this is a crucial dimension to the show, but there are other features that slightly complicate the situation and open up other elements of female subjectivity. On the question of power, what transpires as the show progresses is that Offred comes to know her power, which is her power to reproduce. The source of her oppression is, thus, also the source of her power.

The interchange of power between master and slave was famously theorised by G.W.F. Hegel in *The Phenomenology of Spirit* (1807). Hegel does not regard the slave as powerless, and while the master 'wins' the contest, he does not do so without a certain, indeed, radical cost. In other words, something is sacrificed, and the dialectic itself is resolved by this complementary sacrifice, where each side is now fatally estranged from something that was once central to them. While the master forces the slave to do the work, the master then loses the enjoyment and knowledge that work brings. In the limit, the master is evacuated of the very substance of life, reduced to the issuing of orders and the grim solace that he might, in the limit, destroy the slave, while realising that he is utterly helpless without the slave. One sees in Hegel's dialectic of the master and the slave, an echo of the famous exchange between Jesus and Pontius Pilate, where the latter is increasingly perplexed by the answers that Jesus gives. The scandal becomes not that the slave is powerless, but that the slave seems to know things that the master cannot.

What *The Handmaid's Tale* does is rework this dialectic (master–slave) at the level of sexual relations and gendered division. Indeed, what is clear is that the handmaid becomes a kind of reparative intermediary that compensates for the impotence of the socially endorsed sexual relation. It transpires as the show moves on that not only the wife, but also the commander, are infertile. To spare the commander from discovering his impotence, Offred begins an affair with Nick, the commander's handsome driver, in the hopes she might fall pregnant to him and pass this child off as the legitimate offspring of the commander.

Moreover, because the handmaids are kept in the house as servants, they are the subject of deep resentment from the wives of the commanders. Indeed, for Serena Joy, her position behind Offred during The Ceremony makes it painfully clear that, in many respects, it is she (the wife) who has been cast into the position of the handmaiden to the sexual act. The Ceremony, in fact, ruthlessly exposes her position as wife as having no grounding in sexual reality. What The Ceremony acts out as a kind of grotesque diorama is a split in femininity between the wife, who occupies the symbolic position of matriarch (feminine legitimacy) and is responsible for the raising of children, and the handmaid, who does the actual 'work' of sex and childbearing.

Melodrama

While the sexual torture of women provides *The Handmaid's Tale* with its moral framework, what takes place at the level of the narrative is best characterised as melodrama. A melodrama was the name given to a variety of musical theatre in the eighteenth and nineteenth centuries. The words were spoken rather than sung, as in opera or operetta, but were accompanied by music played by an orchestra. The music offered the affective register of the action on the stage, modulating from urgent to contemplative, joyous to lugubrious, as the situation changed. This pattern was adopted by early cinema, with films accompanied by scored music played live in the theatre. The music helped compensate for the film's silence, which prevailed until 'talkies' emerged in the late 1920s.

But even with the advent of synchronous sound-tracks in cinema, music was retained as the complement of action. Interestingly, the presence of extra-diegetic music floating through a film does not rupture the realist illusion, but rather seems to somehow reinforce the substance of the action. With television, once again music was a central feature of its dramas, but it was also central to other kinds of programming. Today, music will accompany news documentaries, particularly those with a 'human interest' angle, as well as reality programs like cooking contests or renovation rescues. Shows like *Survivor* (2000–) and *The Amazing Race* (2001–) pulse with relentlessly per-cussive soundtracks drawn from cinematic thrillers and action movies.

In this formal sense, by incorporating extradiegetic music into its dramas, television is by and large melodramatic. But the term 'melodrama' has also come to denote a certain form of female-centred serial, such as the daytime soap operas that follow the lives and loves of characters in the dilated temporality of daily life. The primary aim of a melodrama is the expression of emotions, especially those attached to the anguish felt in one's personal life, such as the travails of love, and the rivalries within families and workplaces. The melodrama is particularly fond of family businesses, which are imagined in quasi-aristocratic terms as 'empires' (*Dallas, Dynasty, The Bold and the Beautiful, Empire*), in which the characters play as kings and queens, heirs and heiresses, courtiers and courtesans. A key feature of the melodrama is the central role allocated to women, who constitute the emotional and agential core of the narratives, rather than acting as mere ancillaries or 'love interests'.

The melodramatic heroine, typically, wants to 'have it all', but is met with the constraints of a hostile and predatory world. In this respect, Offred in *The Handmaid's Tale* is in many ways exemplary. Despite her victimisation at the hands of Commander Waterford and Serena Joy, and the horrific precarity of her life and those of her fellow female slaves, Offred wins most of her contests. The commander, who is not as zealously committed to the regime as some in the ruling party, takes a shine to Offred and they share surreptitious evening meetings playing boardgames and exchanging sly repartee. Serena Joy, who is brutal in her treatment of Offred, also comes to hold her in grudging respect, and is often shown to envy, as strange as it sounds, Offred's freedom. The driver Nick, while not a slave, and enjoying the basic privileges of being male in this world, is still in the position of the subaltern. He, too, is drawn to Offred and they become lovers and uneasy confidantes, never quite knowing whether the other might rat them out.

In this respect, the series has an 'upstairs, downstairs' quality, where the lives of the servants (slaves) are intercut with the lives of the masters. Meanwhile, in free Canada, Offred's husband is working to rescue his wife and their daughter (who has been placed in another wealthy household) from the clutches of Gilead. Offred emerges in all this as a woman who, after a fashion, has it all. Formally barred from society's upper echelons, she nevertheless enjoys a privileged intimacy with both the commander and the wife, who take her into their confidence and admire (envy) her self-possession in the face of her oppression. In the end, Offred is the custodian of the sex that they cannot have.

Even so, this special relationship that Offred enjoys with the great and the good does not diminish her loyalty to her class, and she becomes a leader in their resistance movement. Her sexual relationship with Nick is also dignified by the political intrigue of their revolutionary impulses. Through all of this she loses, but also somehow doesn't lose, her actual conventional family: a loving husband and a beautiful daughter. Offred never fails to win and retain the adoration of those she encounters, who see something unique, special and powerful in her, qualities never quite belied by her apparently abject status as handmaiden. In this respect, we can see that the melodrama, even one with a direct political critique, is also a working out of the master-slave dialectic that transects the very heart of feminine subjectivity and which revolves around the quandary of feminine power.

The Hunger Games

Another popular variant of contemporary dystopian stories is that based around sadistic fights to the death, such as in *The Hunger Games* (2012, 2013, 2014, 2015) film franchise and the book series it draws upon. In this scenario, a perverse and decadent aristocracy stages a contest between selected members of the underclass, not unlike the gladiators of classical times. The contestants must fight each other to the death, performing in a series of contests and trials for the delectation of their overlords. Only the winner will escape with their life. Bearing a resemblance to the contest shows that have come to dominate reality television dramas, stories like *The Hunger Games* take the symbolic 'survival' of contestants in contemporary game shows into the literal level of mortal conflict. What is interesting is how short a step it is. In shows like *Big Brother* or *MasterChef*, when contestants lose or are voted off the show, the remaining (surviving) members of the community enter a period of mourning, crying passionately before the camera and speaking wistfully of the wonderful memories they will retain of the departed. The producers may even proffer a musical montage of their 'life' on the show in tribute.

In the case of *The Hunger Games*, we can also see that the contest format is not incompatible with the modality of melodrama. Like Offred in *The Handmaid's Tale*, Katniss Everdeen, the heroine of *The Hunger Games*, is also a woman who manages to have it all. Interestingly, rather than the sadistic torment of the games played by the ruling class signalling the end of the prospects for Offred and Katniss, it is instead their involvement in this obscene pageant that opens them up to the world of genuine enjoyment. In this respect, these stories resemble the pattern visible in classical *bildungsromane*, such as Stendhal's great novel *The Red and the Black* (1830). In that novel, Julien Sorel, the son of a carpenter, is plucked from obscurity and, through a mixture of his singular personal attributes (beauty, intelligence, force of character) and fortunate patronage, finds himself absorbed into the highest echelons of church and state. Women and men fall in love with him, and his status moves by turns from pet to pawn to protégé. Like Offred and Katniss, Julien Sorel is persecuted and belittled ruthlessly, but always wins the hearts of those above him in the end.

Squid Game

A recent example of the game show dystopia is the Korean Netflix drama *Squid Game* (2021), which captured the global imagination. In this show, the hero, Seong Gi-hun, is also a struggling member of the underclass who is inveigled into a bizarre contest to the death. On the face of it, there are a couple of apparently consequential differences between *Squid Game* and the dystopian texts considered previously. In the first instance, the show is not set in the near future or an alternative present, but in today's Seoul, where Gi-hun is pushing middle age, but still lives a hand-to-mouth existence in his mother's apartment. The game takes place in a secret underground compound hidden on a remote island.

Perhaps the more significant difference, though, is in the character of Gi-hun. Unlike Offred, Katniss and Julien Sorel, Gi-hun is not a beautiful soul who others fall in love with and esteem. Gi-hun is, instead, a rather reprehensible figure, who cannot hold down a job, leeches shamelessly from his ailing mother and gambles away the money he should be giving to his ex-wife as support for their child. In terms of literary types, Gi-hun is best understood as a 'picaro', like Huck in Mark Twain's *Huckleberry Finn* (1884), someone at the bottom of society who lives by their wits and tumbles from one sticky situation to the next.

When Gi-hun at last reaches his limit, having exhausted the patience and livelihoods of those close to him, he is met by an enigmatic stranger who offers him a way out of his impoverished existence. Picked up in the dead of night by a nondescript van, and ushered in by guards in red tracksuits and wearing strange masks emblazoned with geometrical shapes, Gi-hun is drugged and wakes to find himself in what looks like a large gymnasium-cum-dormitory with 456 other 'contestants'. Each is dressed in identical green tracksuits with their number printed on it. Gi-hun, as it happens, is the last contestant and wears the number 456. A faceless voice explains that the winner will take home

Squid Game courtesy of Netflix.

₩4.56 billion (about USD$5 million). The only catch, and this isn't made clear at the outset, is that the contests are fatal. In the first game, 'Red Light, Green Light', 255 people are killed. When the traumatised survivors return to their dormitory, they demand to be let free. A vote is taken, and the survivors vote, very narrowly, to leave the game. Already, it is somewhat of a shock that so many, having watched and only barely survived the initial massacre, voted to go on. Gi-hun votes to leave, disgusted by the carnage, showing that he is not all bad.

Yet, when they are released, one by one the erstwhile contestants find themselves back in the jaws of the very dilemmas that had sent them to the game in the first place. Though they now know its lethal dimension, the extremity of their respective situations forces their hands and they end up asking to be allowed back into the game. Because it focused on the desperation of the poor in wealthy capitalist Korea, *Squid Game* was widely interpreted as a critique of the relentless competition that capitalism institutes as its founding virtue. *Squid Game* came in the wake of *Parasite* (2019), winner of both the Palm d'Or (2019) and the Oscar for Best Picture (2020), which was also a Korean surrealist horror focused on wealth disparity. The director of *Squid Game,* Hwang Dong-yuk, explained that the show was allegorical of the dog-eat-dog nature of capitalist modernity, and that we do after all live in a kind of 'hunger games' with very real winners and very real losers.

The social contract

Despite its baroque premise, *Squid Game* does seek to answer a perplexing question, which is if capitalism really is so evil, why don't we just get rid of it? In the US, the wealthiest 1%

controls more wealth than the middle 60%, so why don't the latter simply vote to redistribute the wealth? Instead, time and again, suggestions to even slightly mitigate wealth inequality are voted down by populaces who plainly suffer under an unjust system. The show directly addresses the 'voluntary' element of social complicity. In the show, the contestants cannot say, 'I didn't sign up for this!' because this is exactly what they did sign up for. When the horrific nature of the game is made plain, they still choose to remain. So, when the 'masters' of this murderous game are asked 'why are you doing this to us?' their answer is to say 'we have not compelled anyone to be here'.

Here we can see how contemporary dystopia is locked in a singular orbit around the enigma of choice. Choice is at the heart of the prestige of liberal capitalism, where citizen consumers enjoy freedoms of speech, association, movement, religion, sexuality and so on. This freedom of choice is understood, not always consciously, as the correlate of the choice enjoyed as consumers, where capitalist markets produce a dizzying choice of products. We choose our political leaders, and we choose our hair conditioner, we choose our jobs and our life partners. Thus, in dystopias, what seems to disappear is choice, and in its place, what emerges is compulsion. Or sometimes, as in *Squid Game*, we get something more precise, which is that the desperate contestants 'choose' to remain in a game that enforces its rules and its outcomes with deadly force, and where there can be only one winner.

Of course, the immediate answer is that the situation in *Squid Game* illustrates exactly that such decisions are not freely arrived upon but made under extreme duress. In Rousseau's *The Social Contract* (1762), a key treatise in both the French and American Revolutions, it was argued that political legitimacy was conferred by an implicit agreement between a government and its citizens. While none of us remember actually signing any such agreement, we still entertain this idea as foundational of the liberal order. At the heart of *Squid Game* is a fundamental ambiguity. On the one hand, it shows very clearly that the contestants have little choice when they make their fatal decision to return to the game. But, on the other hand, they still do have a choice. Each could have stayed and faced the music in their outside life – expulsion from the country, going to prison, letting their ill mother go untreated. In other words, despite the overwhelming reasons to join the murderous game, there remains a traumatic kernel of agency.

In many ways, in fact, *Squid Game* bears a strong structural (and even visual) resemblance to the seminal Netflix drama *Orange is the New Black* (2013–19). In both cases we are in a prison with armed guards, prisoners in coloured uniforms, and tightly regulated daily life (food, time). As an aside, we can note a resemblance here to the way that time was once more strictly timetabled in the heyday of broadcast television. The prison also gives us the basic set-up of a world inside and a world outside; that is to say, we are presented with a split diegesis (the notional world on the screen). In both series, there is a marked ambiguity in which it is genuinely open to question which of these two places (inside or outside) is 'hell'. Moreover, in both *Squid Game* and *Orange is the New Black,* we have that now-familiar structure that was pioneered in the show *Lost* (2004–10) of ensemble cast and backstory. In terms of a temporality, the ensemble cast is together in the 'now', and separated once again in the 'then' of their backstory flashback. Each backstory is a replaying of the particular circumstances that have led each character to their current situation (magical island, women's prison, dystopian hunger game). Another way to put this is to say that each backstory takes us to the primal scene that constitutes the character in question.

The master's pleasure

One interesting difference in *Squid Game*, though, is the particular role assigned to the masters. In *Orange is the New Black*, there is a moment in the series where the running of the prison is contracted out to a private 'service provider' and everything in the prison, which was thought to be already pretty bad, becomes inexorably worse. The collective life that used to take place in the kitchen, where prisoners cooked meals, is taken away because it's cheaper to send in pre-prepared bulk food from outside and just heat it up. But we never really see the true or ultimate master in *Orange is the New Black* because, in the end, who is the true master in the capitalist order?

If we credit the idea of a social contract underpinned by free and fair elections and constitutionally guaranteed rights, then we must say that the 'master' is us. Yet, most of us would recoil immediately from that suggestion – no, the master is someone else, I am just an ordinary person, I don't make the rules and so on. In *Squid Game*, we do see the master, although he remains masked for much of the program. In this respect, the masked master precisely captures the condition of mastery in capitalism, which has its strict rules but no actual monarch to issue them.

But what is the essential element that the master possesses? At first glance, one would say the master has power. But *Squid Game* is very clear that the true answer is that the master has pleasure. The game has been organised for the pleasure of the master. Interestingly, even before we are shown the master, we know that he must be there enjoying. Why? Because the games are perverse. They are all variations of childhood games, elaborately staged in garish colours, and with visual non-sequiturs drawn from M.C. Escher and René Magritte. What has made these childhood games so terrifying? In the first instance, there is the entry of death, not as a childish abstraction, but as a point of true finality. But concomitant with this is the transference of pleasure from the participants, who are now in abject terror, to the game itself. In other words: I am not enjoying the game; the game is enjoying me.

In this way, *Squid Game*, which presents itself as an allegory of capitalist exploitation, comes to revolve very strictly around the enigma of the master's enjoyment. Of course, as with all television, and popular culture more generally, we have to also factor in the central dimension of our enjoyment. In other words, if the master is getting off by watching his desperate contestants suffer, why do we get pleasure from watching him watching them? Indeed, are we not, through the agency of the camera, directly aligned with the master watching in rapt fascination as the horrors unfold? Thus, horrific shows like *The Handmaid's Tale* and *Squid Game* carry with them their own implicit scandal, which is the fact that these programs only exist because they are enjoyed by their audiences. Squaring the dimension of enjoyment with the framework of political critique is the central problem of dystopian narratives.

Chapter Two

Amnesia

In the Introduction, I suggested that streamed television decoupled television drama from the time of social life by removing it from the framework of broadcasting schedules. The changed relationship to time that on-demand viewing instils has its correlate in the theme of memory that so strongly marks contemporary television. We now live in an age where nothing is forgotten, where every email and social media post is retained somewhere in the cloud, where newspapers no longer decay and disappear, but sit permanently in a vast archive, and where even the dead persist in profiles that no one feels quite authorised to remove. Given we now live surrounded by this ever-growing archive, it is something of a paradox that memories seem more elusive than ever. The evanescence of memory finds a particular expression in the amnesia plot, where a character loses their memory. But where have their memories gone? And why have they departed? They seem to have disappeared somewhere inside of the amnesiac, frustratingly beyond their recall. But they return in two forms. Firstly, in the form of the traumatic fragment, suddenly and seemingly without context. And secondly, they reappear in the form of a situation, as if the world has decided to act out their lost memory for them.

I May Destroy You

The award-winning series *I May Destroy You* (2020) follows a group of young Black artists living in contemporary London. The show's heroine, Arabella, played by the creator and director of the series Michaela Coel, is an aspiring writer. Arabella's successful blog was converted into a hit book and she is now struggling to write her second book. She has been given an advance, which she has spent, but the book is far from finished and the publishers are beginning to get anxious, trying to 'support' her to get it done. Arabella's best friends are Terry, a struggling actor, and Kwame, an aerobics instructor. The *mise-en-scène* is the bars, cafés, share houses and yoga studios of semi-bohemian London. Arabella, Terry and Kwame are all rather hopelessly lost and it is not immediately obvious how they will find their way, since even success only seems to redouble their plight by making them feel ever more fraudulent and hollow.

Once upon a time, a confused and aimless character teetering on the cusp of adulthood would have been dutifully absorbed by the narrative machinery known as the *bildungsroman*, which we touched on in the last chapter. In the *bildungsroman* (education novel), we watch a character come of age. They go through a series of struggles, their youthful vanities come up against the sharp imperatives of social existence, and they learn the bitter lessons that will set them on their course to a viable adulthood. Isn't this exactly what is happening in *I May Destroy You*? In some ways, yes. Arabella is learning about work, relationships, the true sources of self-esteem, the regulation of pleasure, and how to cope with loss and disappointment. The show follows the painful journey of Arabella and her friends through these situations. One might even observe that *I May Destroy You* is a subspecies of the *bildungsroman* known as the *künstlerroman*, which documents the emergence of the artist, as in Willa Cather's *The Song of the Lark* (1915) or James Joyce's *A Portrait of the Artist as a Young Man* (1916).

What typifies the particular moment we live in, however, is the way that the *bildungsroman* collides with another narrative form, which is the amnesia story. The amnesia plot, whereby a protagonist loses their memory and spends the film trying to piece their life back together, is not in itself new. Indeed, it has a venerable history within cinema. Films with this premise date back to the 1910s and there was a spate of amnesia films in the 1940s, with Hitchcock's *Spellbound* (1945) an exemplary case. The amnesia premise strongly re-emerged at the turn of the millennium (*Memento* [2000], *Mulholland Drive* [2001]) and it remains a popular device in both cinematic and televisual drama. With the advent of the digital age, memory becomes inflected with the qualities of data storage that are at the heart of contemporary computing. The idea that our own memories might consist of 'files' that can be stored, deleted, copied, compressed, corrupted and so on is an inevitable result of this implied analogy. Something of this phenomenon can be seen in *I May Destroy You*.

The scanner fails

The central event of *I May Destroy You* is Arabella's sexual assault in a toilet after being drugged in a bar. Because she was drugged, she cannot remember anything of the event, including the identity of the perpetrator. She wakes up the next day, and though she is alone in her own bed, she knows immediately that she has been raped. The memory comes to her in flashes, but the crucial elements lie frustratingly beyond reach. She reports the assault to the police and is medically examined, where the rape is confirmed. Though the police are sympathetic, and do not fundamentally doubt her story, they are not able to progress the investigation because Arabella can recall neither who she was with nor where it happened.

Arabella's response is to dissociate. She knows that she was assaulted but proceeds as if she has not been. The event is incommensurate with her life, which is another way to define the traumatic. The assault she suffers seems specifically formulated to flummox the *bildungsroman*. In the *bildungsroman*, suffering happens in series and leads to growth. The contemporary impediments, however, are not redeemable through incremental learning, but situated in the direct quandary of a foundational trauma. This is not to trivialise sexual assault, but rather to place it in a certain historical moment. It allows us to see the function that (non-) memory has in contemporary cultural narratives. Amnesia signals the moment in the text where the subject (the hero of the narrative) is formed, and in structural terms, gives expression to the traumatic intrusion of sexuality.

In one intercut sequence, we see two alternate scenes. In the first scene, Arabella is talking with a counsellor in the wake of her sexual assault. In the other scene, we see her friend Kwame having casual sex with a male stranger in a public toilet. There is a formal realism in both scenes, which we experience as grittiness and sitting within the traditions of British cinematic realism. The lighting is grim, and the cameras low and jumpy. For scenes that depict, respectively, the moment and the aftermath of sex (albeit in one case the sex is consensual and in the other it is non-consensual), what stands out is the absence of stylisation. The sex is stripped of the usual niceties of on-screen lovemaking, and the counselling session is staged awkwardly in a bare room with a low ceiling. In both situations, functionality has almost fully displaced the manners that provide the basis for intimacy.

In fact, for people who pride themselves on their creativity, we are left a little shocked by the highly instrumentalised quality of the lives that Arabella and Kwame live. The overwhelming sense is of things being perfunctory, of just getting it over and done with and moving on to the next task. Immediately after the sex act concludes, we see the two men washing their hands and leaving the toilet without speaking to each other. In the next scene, Kwame is being served by this same man in the supermarket, where he works at the cash register. There is no acknowledgement of the intimate act that they shared moments earlier. The man scans Kwame's items mechanically and moves on to the next customer. In the counselling room, Arabella demands her therapist fix her, implying she is busy and needs to get on with her life. She has a book to write and does not have time for boomer introspection and other tiresome rituals. In effect, and with little sense of how insulting she is being, Arabella tells the counsellor that *if you can't fix me this instant, what is the point of you?*

Both scenes (Kwame's sexual encounter and Arabella's counselling session) are crying out for gravity, for dignity, or simply the expressive dimension that is the usual province of melodrama. Intercut sequences always imply a kind of relationship, so the sequence opens up a relationship between these two moments: Kwame in the toilet and Arabella in therapy. What is sad about each is not the act itself, as the act is real enough. What is sad is the radical alienation that Kwame and Arabella have from their interior lives, from themselves. It is significant that, in each case, their alienation revolves around sex, and that the black hole in each moment is the male public toilet. One of the only memories that Arabella has of her assault is that it took place in a public toilet, and this place seems to stand for the opacity of male desire. The toilet is where men go to fulfil their most secret desires and excrete their shameful waste. In the show, there is an obscene equivalence (relationship) drawn between the male toilet and the female body. For a woman, they represent the battleground of their subjectivity, the place where any lasting independence must be won.

Going viral

Arabella attempts to deal with her trauma in various ways. On the one hand, she tries to ignore it – she throws herself back into her life, and tells her friends she is fine. At the same time, she treats it as something she will get to later, once she has dealt with the more immediate problem of her unwritten book. Yet, when she tries to write this book, she finds that she is 'blocked'. On the other hand, Arabella also tries to reinhabit the life she had before the assault, which has taken on a prelapsarian glow. At one point Arabella decides suddenly, even though she is virtually broke, to return to Italy, where she had a short-lived romance with an Italian man while on holiday. Unsurprisingly, when she turns up unannounced, the man is mortified and locks her out of his apartment and tells her to leave him alone.

Arabella then 'acts out' the trauma, which is to say, she repeats it. This takes an intriguing and insidious form in the story. Her concerned publisher assigns her a mentor named Zain to help coax her through her writer's block. Zain is attractive and charming, roughly the same age as Arabella, and they fall into a sexual relationship. After sex, she discovers that Zain is no longer wearing the condom that he was when the sex commenced. Zain puts it down to an accident, and Arabella thinks nothing more of it. Yet, the next morning, Arabella happens to catch a podcast (summoning this exact message from the cloud) of women talking about how men will cunningly remove condoms during sex – a well-known technique of predatory males.

I May Destroy You courtesy of BINGE and HBO.

Her lover Zain even uses the same excuses that have been formulated by these men.

At a publishing event, and with a large crowd assembled, Arabella breaks away from her prepared speech to say that she has been violated by Zain, leaving her audience in shocked silence. Videos of this dramatic moment quickly go viral, and Arabella is lauded for courageously exposing Zain's abusive behaviour. And yet, this seeming victory does not resolve Arabella's situation. Within a certain narrative logic it would, since Arabella has 'taken control' of the story and wrenched away the veil of secrecy that allows abuse to flourish. So, why was Arabella still stuck? What the show dramatises is that acting out a change does not necessarily institute a change. Nor, it seems, does claiming the high ground on social media.

The primal screen

I May Destroy You is eloquent on the dilemmas of contemporary mediated life. When Arabella is forced to be by herself, like many of us, she reaches for her phone. Immediately upon waking up, or finishing a meal, even after sex, the phone will come out. The morning after Arabella has sex with Zain is filmed in an uncharacteristically joyous fashion. Sun streams into her apartment and Arabella bounces out of bed to start her morning yoga routine. There is light-hearted banter with Zain as he wanders through to have a shower. Separated from the open plan apartment by frosted glass, we hear the warm water splash merrily on the screen and see the shadow of his body as he washes. We also see Arabella's body casually contorted into various yoga shapes as she flicks through her social media and watches her favourite programs.

Checking the phone when one wakes up has largely taken the place of reading the newspaper in the morning or turning on the radio or television. But social media is not quite the same as the traditional public media of print, television and radio. Social media (re)introduces a fundamental ambiguity between the public and the private. Unlike television and cinema, social media allows us to participate in the screen life of the social world. Yet, on the other hand, it also allows the social world to participate in the screen life of our subjectivity. Arabella is emblematic of the new compulsion to find subjective confirmation in social media. In her case, it has, in fact, opened the pathway to success. She won a book contract because of the popularity of her blog *Confessions of a Fed-up Millennial*, which specialised in channelling youthful discontentment in a sassy way. Her first book was a compilation of her posts. The new book is meant to be different, and yet Arabella cannot write it.

It is commonplace today to note the proliferation of screens in daily life, but what *I May Destroy You* dramatises is not so much the multiplication of screens but their collapse. This raises the question of the function of a screen. This is a complex phenomenology because it seems that different screens (for example, a cinema screen, a television screen, an ATM screen) are doing different things. Screens are generally imagined as a surface on which something is projected or displayed. But it is also important to recognise the earlier sense in which screens were used as veils and dividers, such as the screen that separates the two people in the Catholic practice of confession. This veiling and dividing function does not, in fact, disappear with the advent of the cinematic screen. Merely because we project something onto a screen does not mean that we are not also, at the same time, screening something off.

We can see something of the radical character that screens have in the social field of the digital age when we look again at the scene in *I May Destroy You* taking place the morning after Arabella has sex with Zain. There are at least five screens that are active in the sequence. First, there is the one that we (the audience) are watching, the one which we treat as a kind of window that allows us into the imagined world of Arabella and her friends. Second, there is the screen that Arabella is watching on her phone and which she uses to access the public sphere: podcasts, socials, texts, emails. The third, less obvious, screen is Arabella's own body which she maintains with a dedication not seen in any other activity. The fourth screen is the shower screen concealing Zain, which like the male public toilet, is the one that signifies the opacity of male desire.

The fifth screen is completely invisible, but is the most critical; namely, the psychic screen that separates Arabella from her traumatic moment. It is this invisible screen that conditions the entire narrative and makes Arabella act in the way she does. In the show, this last screen (the primal screen) is given visual expression through Arabella's bed. In effect, what happens on top of the bed acts out the contents of what is below the bed; that is, what Arabella hides under her bed is the consequences of what happens on the bed. At one point, Arabella rummages underneath her bed and we see a bag containing bloody tissues and an ultrasound image of a foetus. Nowhere does Arabella speak of this presumed pregnancy or her desire for a child. That entire dimension of her subjective structure exists only in the image of the rubbish she cannot throw away and must keep beneath her bed. This also highlights another key dimension of a screen. Against the common idea that the screen is a place where one escapes, we need to place the idea that the screen is the intimate field where things emerge. Only this explains why social media is such a site of ambivalence, and why people need to take a break from it or enter a period of 'digital detox'. The emergent, eruptive dimension of the screen is acted out very clearly in the 'morning after' scene with Zain. Zain *emerges* from the shower, the podcast on condom removal *emerges* from Arabella's phone, and Arabella *emerges* from the stylisation of her body, destitute except for Zain's shirt. And in the wake of this, the show itself emerges from its Hollywood afterglow and back into its grimy British realism.

Homecoming

Another exemplary amnesia text is Amazon Prime's conspiracy thriller *Homecoming* (2018–20). Instead of the trauma of sexual assault that animates *I May Destroy You*, *Homecoming* is concerned with the trauma of war. In this respect, we can see that each program is situated in the trauma considered most distinctive of each gender. In *Homecoming*, a group of American soldiers return from their tours of duty in Iraq and are placed in the 'Homecoming Transition Support Centre'. The ostensible aim of the Homecoming Centre is to help traumatised or war-affected soldiers transition to civilian life. It is a six-week program, and the soldiers reside at the facility during their treatment.

During the day, they have counselling sessions with the director of the centre, Heidi Bergman (played by Julia Roberts) and they also do group activities that simulate life in the normal world, like working in a shoe store or going to a dinner party. The hero is an earnest young soldier, Walter Cruz, who has returned from service in Iraq. Walter is troubled by the death of a fellow soldier, Lesky. Walter unwittingly sent Lesky to his death by ordering him to ride in a separate vehicle, which was blown up by a roadside bomb. In Walter's sessions with Heidi, she explains that Lesky's death is not his fault, which he knows to be true by most measures, but still cannot escape a feeling of culpability.

While Walter undertakes the treatment in good faith, the other soldiers treat it as just another lame work exercise and goof around during the group activities. However, one of Walter's friends, Joseph Shrier, becomes convinced that the whole operation is a scam. He points out that it is not quite clear whether the soldiers are there freely or compulsorily. While they are there at their own volition, no one has actually tried to leave. Shrier is not even sure they are in Florida, as they have been told. As well as the too-good-to-be-true friendliness of the centre, and the suspicions of Shrier, the sinister dimension of the Homecoming Centre is also foreshadowed by the phone calls that Heidi Bergman has with her boss, Colin Belfast. In these exchanges, Colin is hectoring and threatening, continuously emphasising that there is a lot at stake and that Geist needs 'good results' to pitch for a full contract with the Department of Defence.

A split in time

The most distinctive element of *Homecoming*, however, is the way the action switches between two storylines that are differentiated by their visual appearance. The first storyline is the one taking place at the Centre, which looks very much like the present day, with the neutral interior spaces of a contemporary medical centre or professional firm. The colours are sharp, the surfaces shiny and the aspect ratio is 16:9, which, as we saw with *WandaVision*, became standard with the introduction of digital television in the late 1990s. There is then a second storyline, which is projected in the old boxy 4:3 ratio. In this plot we are no longer in the shiny open spaces of the Homecoming Centre, but in the 'outside' world of contemporary America, with its diners and strip malls and everyday mess. Although we recognise a number of the characters, the colours are more washed out and grainy, and the clothes and settings look older. This, along with the squarer aspect ratio, signal that we have gone into the past, flashing back to an earlier period.

This assumption is reinforced by the fact that the characters we have met in the Homecoming Centre evince no knowledge of having been there. In other words, they display the unwitting ignorance that the past always has to the future. However, this is all a carefully constructed trap, because it eventually becomes plain that what we took to be the past – that is, the grimy outside world – is in fact the future. The reason why the characters in this timeline have no knowledge of the Homecoming Centre is not because it has not happened yet, but because they have lost their memories as a result of being administered an experimental drug developed by the Geist company. The drug has been designed to remove soldiers' traumatic war memories so that they can be more quickly recycled back into military service.

The other has an other

Homecoming has the familiar paranoid structure of the political thriller or espionage drama, exemplified in recent years by the Jason Bourne film franchise, and prominent during

Cold War–era films like *The Manchurian Candidate* (1962) or Hitchcock's *North by Northwest* (1959). The paranoid formula is 'the other has an other'. The paranoid person never believes that it is really you that they are talking to, but rather someone behind you who is pulling the strings and has a secret, malevolent agenda. In this case, the kindly face and empathetic demeanour of Heidi Bergman is a 'front' for the brutal instrumentalism of her boss, Colin Belfast. But the paranoid structure is regressive, for as soon as you unveil the person behind the person, the paranoiac immediately discerns that there is indeed someone who is behind *them*. The only thing that stays constant is the aim of the other's other, which is without fail to persecute, violate and exploit the subject.

In the paranoid film, the world is always shadowy, inhabiting a prism of deception where nothing ever lines up. The hero of such films is a dupe, the unwitting victim of an elaborate conspiracy. In *Homecoming*, it is Walter Cruz who performs the role of the trusting, gullible subject. Walter downplays the concerns of his paranoid friend Shrier, and offers plausible explanations for the various inconsistencies that emerge. Above all, he trusts Heidi and, in this respect, the show follows the outlines of *film noir*, which also plays to a paranoid structure. In *film noir*, a hard-bitten male protagonist thinks they have the measure of the world and prides themselves on trusting no one. However, their defences are breached by the arrival of a *femme fatale*. This woman presents initially as a damsel in distress, and the hero is lulled into the fantasy that he is saving her, only to find that she is not quite what she seems. In this way, the *femme fatale* acts as the feminine hinge of the conspiracy.

Yet, while the hero in the paranoid world of the political thriller is a dupe, he is never quite innocent. There are some similarities here with the story of sexual violation, where the traumatic dimension comes precisely from the suspicion that somewhere in the chain of events hides the tiniest trace of complicity. It does not matter that no reasonable person would consider them guilty. If that were all that was at stake, neither Arabella nor Walter would be so stuck in their memories. For Walter Cruz, his actions were seemingly innocent. He could not have known that Lesky's vehicle would have been the one to hit the explosive device in Iraq; the bomb could just as easily have struck Walter's vehicle. On the other hand, Walter was the commanding officer and he was the one the who ordered Lesky to ride separately.

Moreover, the motives for this order were a little less than pure, and this emerges as Walter talks to Heidi during their sessions. Lesky had been getting on people's nerves, but his mixture of gullibility and indignation made for good sport in Walter's platoon. Walter had allowed this to happen, and even been party to what he thought was the run-of-the-mill byplay of young men who were, after all, living a life of extreme danger. So, while rationally Walter was not culpable, at an unconscious level, the situation was that he had, in the most basic terms, killed his own brother. This extreme polarisation between innocence and utter responsibility provides the structural complement to the conspiratorial world of the political thriller and its endless shades of guilt and complicity.

The spiral staircase

Into this netherworld stumbles the detective. In *Homecoming* this takes the form of a low-level government official,

Thomas Carrasco, who works in a large bureaucratic department tasked with dealing with complaints. A report had raised concerns about the Homecoming Centre. But when Carrasco raises it with his boss, she dismisses the matter with barely concealed impatience, as if this particular employee were always wasting her time with trifles. (Of course, it turns out that his boss is working for Geist, and is part of the conspiracy.) Carrasco, who mixes self-effacement with a stubborn need to do things by the book, is conflicted. His boss told him unequivocally to drop the matter, but the complaint raised serious questions about the Homecoming Centre.

There is a long scene where Carrasco, almost anonymous in a sea of identical cubicles, stares anxiously through his reading glasses at his screen with his finger poised over his computer mouse. His hair is too neatly combed, and he wears a pressed short-sleeved shirt with pens in the top pocket and an unfashionable tie. On the screen are 'yes' or 'no' buttons that will determine whether the matter is progressed or dismissed. The only sound is a persistent, irritating clicking which we soon find out is Carrasco anxiously clicking his biro in and out. At last Carrasco closes the window on his screen, choosing neither of the options but crucially, keeping the matter alive. He gets out of his chair and walks nonchalantly through the office towards the stairs. His boss, feigning preoccupation with her own work, notices him leave his desk.

When Carrasco reaches the stairwell, the camera offers an overhead shot in which the staircase spirals down into the abyss of the basement. This now archetypal image was made famous in the early film noir *The Spiral Staircase* (1946) and, iconically, in Hitchcock's *Vertigo* (1958). What we are

Homecoming courtesy of Alamy.

meant to experience as Carrasco begins to descend the staircase is the vertigo of the archive, or to put it another way, the archival sublime. The spiral stands for a quite precise experience, insofar as it represents a limit (threshold), which Carrasco is about to fatally cross. And, at the same time, the spiral staircase represents the *absence* of a limit: a fractal reduplication of a fundamental shape, an infinite regress, a curve that never reaches its horizon. This sense of a terrifying, limitless expanse signalled by the spiral staircase is maintained when Carrasco reaches the dimly lit basement where high beige-metal bookcases stretch out in all directions filled with identical folder boxes.

This basement archive, drawing its iconography from the paper era, is the figuration of knowledge in the digital age. The giveaway is not the endless paper files, which like the earnest civil servant marooned amongst them, seem to belong to an earlier epoch. The signal that we are, in fact, in the digital age is that when Carrasco enters the archive, it *knows* he is there. As he walks through the darkened corridors of metal shelving, searching for the number carefully written on a scrap of paper, a solitary overhead sensor light flicks on as he arrives, and off again as he leaves each section. Another overhead shot shows the effect of these automated lights, which flicker on and off to track Carrasco as he beetles his way through the labyrinth of the archive. What we have in this scene is a depiction of knowledge in the digital age, where the key element is not that we know things, but that they know us. We see this now when we look for outdoor furniture in a search engine and immediately find persistent furniture advertisements in our social media feed. It is no longer even uncanny when this happens.

The internet is now integral to our idea of knowledge. After all, we ask the internet questions and it gives us answers. But what does the internet look like? The basement scene in *Homecoming* seems to be trying to picture our idea of the internet, what we imagine to be going on behind the screen, behind the unintelligible lines of code, the torrent of zeros and ones. It is interesting that the status of the archive as a place of knowledge is underpinned by a prohibition. In simple terms, it is illegal to enter the true archive. This illicit dimension is evoked as Carrasco stealthily creeps into the archive, knowing that he could be sprung at any moment.

Select and delete

A key ambiguity of the Homecoming Centre, the one that can be said to be instigating the paranoia, is the question of its therapeutic aim. Is the goal of the therapy the soldiers are receiving to remember or to forget? Within classical psychoanalysis, the answer is clear: the goal is to remember. Freud's famous dictum was that whatever we do not remember we are condemned to repeat; that is to say, to act out or express through our symptoms. In this psychoanalytic context, 'remember' means to accept a memory as one's own and be able to express it in words. Against this process is a diametrically opposed strategy, one which has a much stronger intuitive appeal. Would it not be more logical, after all, if we are traumatised by a memory, to find a way of removing it? This seems a lot cleaner than the psychoanalytic procedure of re-living and re-traumatising the suffering subject.

This fantasy of removing the offending memory seems to owe something of its persistence to the fact that we can remove items from our computer's data storage. The idea formed the premise of Charlie Kaufman's film *Eternal Sunshine of the Spotless Mind* (2004), where a procedure cleansed one's mind of its unpleasant memories. The corollary of this idea can be seen in Ridley Scott's *Blade Runner* (1982) and Christopher Nolan's *Inception* (2010), where memories are not removed but 'implanted'. In *Homecoming* we learn that the goal of Geist and the Homecoming Centre is exactly the same as in Kaufman's suggestive film, which is to erase painful memories. The main difference is the paranoid dimension that we have already noted, and which is introduced through the elements of secrecy and exploitation. Where in *Eternal Sunshine of the Spotless Mind*, the central characters volunteer to have their memories of each other removed following their painful break up, in *Homecoming* the soldiers are being administered the drug without their knowledge. In addition, it is not to help them, but to increase the efficiency of the military.

But how does the drug know which memory to erase? The drug 'knows' because it is not just any old memory, but the memory that presents the subject as an impasse: a thought that cannot be thought past, something that can neither be remembered nor forgotten. In Walter's case, he is trying to forget the death of his friend Lesky. This event is his own foundational crime or original sin. But what happens if this original sin is erased? In the show, the removal of foundational trauma is not an act of liberation or cure, but something altogether more hideous. Even though it is the memory that torments them, forcibly erasing it from their minds takes on the complexion of a deep and intimate violence – indeed, a kind of lobotomy or castration. As Walter starts to lose his memory, he becomes more cheerful and more empty, stripped of his existential gravity. At some level, he is not quite Walter anymore and never will be again. In fact, he seems to have become no one at all. What the show seems to indicate is that the traumatic memory is not something that you can remove without removing the very core of subjective life.

Moreover, removing the memory does not erase the crime, it only causes it to be repeated. The theme of repetition will be addressed in the following chapter, but we can introduce it here by noticing that, in seeking to erase the memory of Walter's own crime, Heidi Bergman commits a new crime. As the cost of the success of the drug becomes visible to Heidi, she is assailed by a terrible guilt, unable to forgive herself for her role in this monstrous operation. Her solution is to take the drug herself, so she will be able to remove her guilt. In her case, she does not become vacant and blithe, which was the fate of Walter, but surly and cynical. She takes a job at a fish shack and goes back to live with her mother. In voluntarily taking the amnesia drug, Heidi opts for the solution that was offered in *Eternal Sunshine of the Spotless Mind*. The result in both cases is the strange situation of an amnesiac love story. Both parties can no longer remember the person they are meeting, nor realise that their meetings are now bound by their mutual amnesia to endless repetition.

We can also see that Heidi's decision to take the amnesia drug is what creates the gap that structures the program, splitting the story into two timelines and two aspect ratios. Eventually, we learn that four years have elapsed between Walter's stay at the Homecoming Centre and the commencement of the investigation by Carrasco. This willed amnesia, a dramatisation of the psychic process of repression, is the basis for the show's constitutive split, preventing its aspect ratios from coinciding and distorting its basic Cartesian coordinates. In each timeline, Heidi is ignorant of her other self and the only thing that will join these two Heidi's together (make them continuous) is remembering the memory she erased. Yet, the only way to integrate that memory is to accept her own role in it.

While outwardly quite different, both *I May Destroy You* and *Homecoming* share key elements that shine a light on the nature of memory and amnesia. They are both, notably, structured by the investigation of a crime. In *Homecoming*, there is the introduction of an external detective in the figure of Carrasco, who doggedly uncovers the Geist conspiracy, and gradually draws the two timelines together. Significantly, this act of suture, stitching together a foundational split, is done in the service of memory and not forgetting. It introduces the work of memory as a positive and fraught process, which stands, somehow, in direct dialectical opposition to the vast and empty memory of the digital archive. In *I May Destroy You*, no external detective takes over the task of finding the criminal. Instead, Arabella herself becomes both the detective and the *femme fatale* in her own *film noir*.

Just like Walter in *Homecoming*, Arabella is also administered a drug without her knowledge to serve the exploitative ends of faceless men. This drug has also caused a very specific amnesia that – just like the one developed by Geist in *Homecoming* – causes her to lose the memory of a traumatic experience. And, as with Walter, the effect of losing this memory for Arabella is a subjective hollowing out. Rather than the cheerful emptiness of Walter, or the bitter emptiness of Heidi, Arabella's emptiness becomes anxiously needful of finding itself mirrored in the illusory affirmations of social media.

Chapter Three

Repetition

Another popular premise to emerge in cinema in recent times is a character who finds themselves trapped in a time loop, endlessly repeating the same day. The film that took this idea into broad public consciousness was the comedy *Groundhog Day* (1993), in which a cynical TV weatherman (played by Bill Murray) wakes each morning to find himself repeating the day he had just lived. Increasingly desperate, he commits suicide in a variety of ways only to find this to no avail. He wakes up each time and it is February 2nd once again. The film's premise struck something in the experience of life, such that the term 'groundhog day' is now a colloquial expression to mean something that repeats endlessly, and where no one ever seems to learn any lessons.

The time loop premise remains popular, visible in recent films like the romantic comedy *Palm Springs* (2020), and science fiction thrillers like *Source Code* (2011), *Edge of Tomorrow* (2014) and *Doctor Strange* (2016). At the end of the last chapter, we saw that the attempt to erase memory (induce amnesia) had the effect of causing a repetition. And indeed, there are films such as *Memento* (2000) and *50 First Dates* (2004) where one character's amnesia creates repetition not dissimilar to the generalised repetition seen in *Groundhog Day*. Within media history, the concept of repetition came into view when popular television series were 'repeated' at less premium times, sometimes during the same week as the initial airing, but sometimes months or years afterwards. The capacity to repeat was personalised with the advent of various technologies, including the VCR machine in the 1980s, the DVD player in the 1990s, and the hard-drive recorder in the 2000s.

Russian Doll

Within streamed television, a prominent example of the repetition device is the dramedy *Russian Doll* (2019–22). The show stars Natasha Lyonne (one of the co-creators) as Nadia Vulvokov, and is set in contemporary bohemian New York City in a milieu that is not too different from the one that Arabella occupies in the London of *I May Destroy You*. The title references both Nadia's Russian heritage and the nested dolls of Russian folk art, which are a kind of popular shorthand for infinite regression. Lyonne, with her large eyes and mass of unruly hair has a certain doll-like Shirley Temple quality; indeed, Nadia's friends often call her 'baby' or 'the baby'. But Nadia's demeanour cuts across these traits, as she smokes and drinks heavily, swears colourfully and has sex with whomever she feels like.

The show begins with a birthday party that Nadia's friends are having for her in a funky city apartment. Nadia has just turned 36 and at the edge of her mind is the sense that her life has really gone nowhere. She protects herself from this sense of emptiness by adopting a swashbuckling nihilism and cynical *c'est la vie* stance towards the world. Like

Phil Connors in *Groundhog Day*, despite her devil-may-care sense of cosmic liberty, Nadia is trapped within the prison of her own cynicism, which is nothing other than a direct expression (as it was for Phil) of the impotence of her life. In the opening scene, Nadia is in the ornate bathroom of her friend's apartment staring at herself in the mirror. Inside the bathroom, Nadia is not cavalier and carefree, but anxious and lost. We find out that by turning 36, she has now surpassed the age her mother died. This is expressed as I have 'outlived my mother', which is an odd choice of phrase, since Nadia's mother had died more than 20 years earlier.

From inside the bathroom, we hear an insistent knocking sound that, in aural terms, is not unlike the clicking sound we heard when Thomas Carrasco was agonising over whether to progress the complaint against Geist in *Homecoming*. In this case, the knocking is actually that of annoyed fellow

Russian Doll courtesy of Netflix.

partygoers who have lined up to use the bathroom. While they have a diegetic source (emitting from the realist situation of the scene), in both examples, the irritating repetitive sound takes on an extradiegetic quality, as if coming from somewhere beyond the visible world of the movie. The ambiguity of this insistent, grating percussion indicates that it is not just the sound of a pen clicking or a door being knocked, but the auditory signal that we are in the presence of repetition.

Time loop

At the party, Nadia meets a self-absorbed English professor and brings him home. On the way, they stop in at a delicatessen where she buys cigarettes and condoms, and asks after Oatmeal, a cat she shares with the deli owner. It is late at night, and the deli is a little raucous with people leaving parties and bars. In the background, she notices a young man vomit and the deli owner tells her he is a friend, and he is going through a rough patch. Later, after she has sex with the professor and sends him on his way, Nadia goes outside to smoke and spots Oatmeal in the park across the street. She steps out onto the road and is instantly killed by a taxi speeding down the road. We see her broken lifeless body sprawled out on the tarmac. Then the screen goes to black and opens again with Nadia staring at herself (at us, in point of fact) in the mirror in the bathroom at her friends' apartment. Thus, the time loop is established in which each time Nadia dies in new and bizarre ways.

The time loop might seem to innately frustrate the progression of a narrative, but the reason that narrative is sustained is due to the fact that Nadia (just like Phil Connors in *Groundhog Day*) remembers the previous iterations of the day. So, here we see that the time loop film is the inverse of the amnesia film. In the amnesia film, the hero forgets a past that everyone else remembers. In the time loop film, the hero remembers a past (each previous iteration of 'the day') that everyone else forgets. What this situation precipitates in the case of both Phil and Nadia is a belated opportunity for growing up. Or to put this in literary terms, it catalyses the *bildungsroman*.

Repetition and learning

Where, in classical *bildungsroman*, a person on the cusp of adulthood moves through misadventures and hardships to maturity, in today's time loop *bildungsroman,* a person on the cusp of middle age is forced to relive the same day over and over again until they accept the reality of their mortal grounding. What is most noticeable in the change is the quality of belatedness that now attaches to the *bildungsroman*. It is as if, in the contemporary moment, it is quite possible to reach one's forties without ever growing up, or even having the faintest clue about what that might mean.

Viewed in this way, and despite the comic nihilism, time loop stories like *Groundhog Day*, *Russian Doll* and *Palm Springs* are distinctly moralistic narrative mechanisms. In essence, they are instructional, following the old injunction to 'do it again until you get it right'. In Phil Connors' case, his world-weary haughtiness masks a paralysing fear of the other. On the day that he is forced to repeat, he is continually assailed by people seeking something from him: a homeless man begs money from him on the street – a long-lost schoolmate tries to sell him life insurance – and he must play his part in the pantomime hokum of the Groundhog Day ritual in Punxsutawney, Pennsylvania.

In the repetition of this day, Phil is forced to contend with the reality of the other. They do not go away, they keep doing what they must always keep doing. The index of Phil's maturation is provided, conventionally enough, by his gradual falling in love with his producer, the *ingénue* Rita (played by Andie MacDowell). By striking out with her time and time again, Phil learns how to woo her. At first this is driven by a calculating need to obtain the erotic object. But, gradually, he comes up against the impasse that he is not going to win any lasting love with a real person in the course of a single day.

In the end, though, there is a breakthrough, and it happens in two ways. In the first instance, Phil starts spending time on learning things and helping people. Of course, each day the person forgets that he had helped them the day before. But Phil doesn't forget, and each new day he helps them in a way that is slightly more meaningful. He learns the piano, and each day he gets better, even though each day is, as it were, his first lesson – which perplexes his teacher. By the end, what Rita sees is not the preening, self-important Phil she is used to, but someone who is esteemed and valued in the community, the very community that she thought Phil had held in contempt.

The second facet of the breakthrough is that Phil gives up on winning over Rita. He finally rests content in the fact that he loves her, and that he has been given the opportunity to love her. What we see in this double movement that releases Phil from the purgatory of repetition is a certain relationship to the object. In giving up his pursuit of Rita, he gives up on the object, allowing it to exist in its state of loss. And, in becoming useful to those around him, he allows himself to be the object. The ethics the film articulates could thus be summarised as follows: objectify oneself and de-objectify the other – do this and you will, against your intuition, gain possession of your life.

Cockroach

Now, if we turn to the case of *Russian Doll,* we can trace a similar process of belated *bildungsroman,* but there are also some key differences. Like Phil, Nadia is alarmed and disbelieving as she realises she is caught in a time loop. At a metaphysical level, we might view the time loop as nothing other than the insistent reminder that death awaits us. And it is also the mechanism by which we learn that death is not, as it is conventionally conceived, the end of things, but in fact, precisely the opposite – it is the frozen unendingness of things. This is the horror that sits underneath both of these comic texts. In case we are not able to grasp that death does not consist in things ending but in their failure to end, both *Groundhog Day* and *Russian Doll* repeatedly demonstrate the impotence of suicide.

In fact, another way of defining Phil's and Nadia's position is that they have been confronted with the impossibility of action. The time loop that incarcerates them is to school them in the necessary preconditions of meaningful action. As well as calling her 'baby', one of Nadia's friends also calls her 'cockroach', telling her in a mixture of admiration and reproach: 'You are a cockroach. Nothing can kill you. You can eat anything, take anything, do anything.' The cockroach is the faunal emblem of the insistence of repetition beyond the end of life. The idea that cockroaches will survive anything took root in the darker days of the Cold War, where it was routinely pointed out that when the entire planet had been blown up, irradiated and plunged into a nuclear winter, cockroaches would still be here. In earlier times, when conjuring death, it was the image of rats and worms gnawing on our corpses that came to mind, now there is the machinic immortality of the cockroach with its brown exoskeleton calmly stalking the lifeless planet.

The desire to know

One of the ways, though, that *Russian Doll* differs from *Groundhog Day* is at the level of knowledge. An unusual feature of the earlier film, at least now looking back, is the surprising equanimity that Phil shows to his fate. He is disturbed, certainly, but does not freak out in the way we might expect when faced with the metaphysical import of his new condition. He is also completely uninterested in the question of why this is happening, what is causing this rupture in space-time. In *Russian Doll*, Nadia reacts more expectedly, and assumes that she is either having a psychotic episode or has reacted very badly to a questionable drug that had been used to spice up the joint she was given as a birthday present.

Nadia also, like Arabella in *I May Destroy You*, becomes a kind of private investigator into her own case. You might even say, she became a very private investigator. (A similar pattern is also visible in the early Netflix superhero series *Jessica Jones* [2015–19].) But unlike Arabella, Nadia seems rather well cast in this role. After all, in her hard-drinking, hard-living cynicism, gravelly New York accent and ubiquitous long coat, Nadia was already styled after the *noir* detective. Thus, her *bildungsroman* must not only be ontologically instituted by a time loop, but epistemologically framed as a detective story. *Russian Doll* shares similarities, in this respect, with *Dirk Gently's Holistic Detective Agency* (2016–17), another metaphysically oriented comic drama. The detective device is often seen as the emblem of rationality, standing in for the scientific method of knowledge that defines modernity. But it is perhaps more precise to lay the emphasis not on the procedure of knowledge (deduction), but on the impetus of knowledge. In this view, the detective is not the emblem of ratiocination, but of the *desire to know*.

Modes of narcissism

Another innovation in *Russian Doll*, when comparing it to the earlier template of *Groundhog Day*, is the introduction of a second, complementary character, Alan Zaveri, who we soon find out is suffering an identical, entwined fate. Alan seems, in many ways, the antithesis of Nadia. Where she lived life recklessly, leaving a trail of destruction, Alan is softly spoken, highly organised and has a compulsive need to control everything. In Nadia's case, we see her desperately trying to shake off the overtures of her former lover, John, a seemingly good man who has left his wife to be with Nadia, only to find himself now spurned. Alan, meanwhile, has summoned the courage to propose to Beatrice, his girlfriend of nine years, only to discover that she is having an affair with her dissertation supervisor, and has been trying to break up with Alan.

The dynamic in this pairing of Nadia and Alan matches that seen between Eleanor Shellstrop (Kristen Bell) and Chidi Anagonye (William Jackson Harper) in the popular series *The Good Place* (2016–20). In *The Good Place*, Eleanor is a deadbeat scoundrel and Chidi is an obsessional philosophy lecturer. It comes as a great shock to Chidi, though, that he has ended up in hell, with all the other terrible people, when in his own mind, all he has ever done is to try to help people and make the world a better place. Just like Eleanor and Chidi, Nadia and Alan represent different modalities of narcissism. Nadia displays a more overt form of narcissism, seemingly only caring about herself, while Alan has that form of selfishness that dresses itself up as a constant, wearying selflessness. He masks his self-absorption as continuous worrying, and a coercive need for things to be just so.

The Rehearsal

If *Russian Doll* enacts repetition in the classical pattern laid down in *Groundhog Day*, a variation on this premise is visible in *The Rehearsal* (2022). This series does not derive its quality of repetition from the time loop premise that animates *Russian Doll*, but instead locates itself within a plausible realist situation. The show presents in the form of a docudrama, in which Nathan Fielder (notionally playing himself) has developed a business that helps clients 'rehearse' potentially problematic situations in advance so that they might better handle the moment when it occurs.

In the first episode, a client named Kor Skeete explains how he has found himself in a fix because he lied about his educational achievements. Kor was part of a team that competed regularly in local quiz nights held at pubs and clubs around town. At one point, his team started discussing their education and it transpired that they had all completed master's degrees. Not wanting to feel left out, Kor also claimed to have a master's degree, although in fact, he only has a bachelor's degree. Since that moment, Kor has felt guilty and fraudulent, which has been made more acute because one member of this group, Tricia, keeps sending him job leads that require the applicant to have a master's degree.

Kor realises he must come clean to Tricia, but is worried about how she might react, and so he has turned to Nathan's firm to help him prepare for this moment. Nathan reassures him that this is exactly what he does, and that they will rehearse the situation (running through all the possible permutations) so that whatever does happen when Kor confesses to Tricia, he will have faced it beforehand and will know exactly what to do. A couple of features stand out already in this situation that differ from *Russian Doll*. First, we seem to have moved from the more grave existential moments that have brought the lives of Nadia and Alan to their point of fatal impasse. Here we have, instead, the normal day-to-day embarrassment of social life, where

The Rehearsal courtesy of BINGE and HBO.

we come up a little short of others' expectations or our own ideals, fluff our lines or put our foot in it. The other key difference is that the very idea of a rehearsal suggests that the repetition is now occurring prior to the potentially traumatic event, rather than in the wake of it.

The Rehearsal begins, as we have noted, in a broadly realist universe, albeit in a register of deadpan satire in which matters are being treated with much more seriousness than they would normally be afforded. Indeed, a third contrast we might notice is that, while Nadia (just like Phil) expounds herself through the dimension of cynicism, Nathan, by contrast, is marked by an extreme credulity and guilelessness. As *The Rehearsal* unfolds, however, it quickly crosses into the realm of absurdity when we see the measures involved in rehearsing Kor's forthcoming confession. In his voiceover narration, Nathan explains that it is critical that the impending encounter between Kor and Tricia be matched to the very last detail. In a warehouse, he constructs a life-sized replica of the bar where the quiz night will take place, and employs a team of actors to act as the bar staff and bar patrons. In the meantime, he orchestrates a meeting between Tricia and the actor he has cast to play her in the rehearsal, so the actor might learn her exact personality, mannerisms and forms of speech.

They begin rehearsing in the replica bar, with Nathan carefully observing Kor's interactions with the actor playing Tricia. Nathan maps their reactions against an intricate flowchart that he has plotted. He notices, at one point, that Kor is becoming distracted by the quiz questions, fretting over the answers and thereby missing golden opportunities to broach his deception with Tricia. It turns out that, while the confession is important, winning the quiz is also important to Kor. Instead of telling Kor to sacrifice the latter goal in favour of the more important task of coming clean with Tricia, Nathan upholds Kor's need to have everything – which is, of course, how Kor landed himself in this mess to begin with.

Nathan goes to great lengths to obtain the quiz show questions in advance from the quiz organisers so that, armed with these answers, Kor would be able to select the right moment to open up to Tricia. However, conscious that Kor would hate to think he gained an unfair advantage, Nathan fixes on a strategy of surreptitiously 'implanting' the answers in Kor's mind without him realising it. Nathan hires yet more actors, and scripts situations that will disclose the answers whilst he and Kor are on a walk to discuss the more general issues of his case. At one point, they stumble upon a crime scene and a police officer (really an actor employed by Nathan) comes out and explains there has been a murder. The officer looks at them bitterly and exclaims: 'It's moments like this that I wish the Chinese had not invented gunpowder.' In this way, and through a series of equally confected moments, Kor is given the answers to the quiz questions in advance and is thereby free to focus on finding the right moment to confess to Tricia.

The structure of anxiety

How might we compare the situations we encounter in time loop narratives like *Russian Doll* with the one we are presented in *The Rehearsal*? As we have already noticed, we seem to have reversed the temporality such that the repetition (now cast as a 'rehearsal') precedes the traumatic moment rather than follows it. But, on the other hand, does it not, after all, result in the same outcome, which is to endlessly repeat the same moment? Moreover, why are we so certain that the time sequence we get is the one that prevails? In other words, are we sure that the rehearsal really precedes the event? In the case of the time loops, we saw that however much they hinged on a past event, they were also urgently directed to the future. Indeed, the temporal ambiguity of the time loop resembles the structure of anxiety. Anxious thinking is directed to a forthcoming event, but that event can only have meaning in relation to something that has already happened. For instance, when facing a driving test, the thought might be: 'I will probably fail *like I always do.*'

It is in this respect that *Russian Doll* and *The Rehearsal* are similar. In the case of Nadia, her point of repetition is caused by the fact that on turning 36 she is now older than her mother was at her early death at 35. As Nadia keeps re-living this day, she is brought closer and closer to the traumatic kernel of her experience, which is that she feels she killed her mother by abandoning her. Nadia's unstable mother had deteriorated to the point where she was genuinely endangering her young daughter, and Nadia was removed from her mother's care.

Although the decision was not Nadia's, who was still a child, the traumatic component is that she is glad to have escaped the terrifying grip of her mother's manipulations and delusions. This foundational disloyalty to her mother in her moment of need (in truth, her mother was always in a moment of need) was brought to its worst end, when her mother died not long afterward. As was the case with Walter Cruz in *Homecoming* or Arabella in *I May Destroy You*, it is irrelevant whether they were actually at fault for their actions (by almost every measure, they are not), what matters is only that the subject unconsciously believes they are guilty. And, in turn, what matters is why they must remain guilty of this crime within the courtroom of their psyche.

Destiny in the digital age

We might now begin to understand the concept of repetition as roughly corresponding to a classical conception of fate or destiny. What is fate, but what cannot be escaped? To be trapped in repetition is to experience one's fate. The main thing that has changed in the current structure of fatality is that the origin of the cause has descended from the realm of the gods and into the primordial dramaturgy of childhood. In the contemporary age, childhood is our Olympus. In Nadia's case, her primordial crime of abandoning (and therefore murdering) her mother is repeated in her pathological fear of attachment, which she tries to camouflage as a celebration of individual freedom. What she cannot bear in John, her good-hearted ex-boyfriend, is that he actually cares for her and takes her much more seriously than she is able to take herself. This is compounded by the fact that John has a daughter, Lucy, who is roughly the same age as Nadia was when she was removed from her mother.

By iterating her day, Nadia gradually realises that she should meet Lucy, as her ex, John, has been asking her to do. After all, Nadia was the catalyst for Lucy's parents separating. But, as the moment approaches, Nadia cannot bring herself to meet the girl. Eventually, though, she finds herself meeting Lucy only for the encounter to take an uncanny turn. As Nadia hands Lucy a book she had found consoling during her own childhood, Lucy morphs into a younger version of Nadia herself. Shocked by this, Nadia undergoes a seizure. Blood starts to spill from Nadia's mouth and, eventually, she coughs up a shard of mirrored glass. In a flashback to Nadia's childhood we had seen how, in a violent rage – indeed, the very one that led to Nadia's removal – her mother smashed every mirror and glass picture frame in their house. This shard of mirror tearing Nadia to shreds from the inside is thus proffered as the image of the murderous maternal, which might be understood as the repressed component of the mother left over after the socially celebrated dimensions (devotion, warmth, selflessness, constancy) are subtracted.

Although one will find nothing so visceral in *The Rehearsal*, with its seemingly inane attempts to prepare for the normal controversies of day-to-day life, in the end the show does follow a similar pattern to that seen in *Russian Doll*. One of the early twists in the program is that we see that 'rehearsing' is not just a service that Nathan provides to others, but a practice he uses in his own life to cope with anxiety. There is a humorous moment, for instance, when we see the initial interview with Kor replayed immediately afterward, this time with an actor playing Kor, and with Nathan earnestly explaining how he had rehearsed the meeting to make sure it went well. The camera pulls back and we see a life-sized replica of Kor's apartment also built in a warehouse. Nathan draws our attention to a slight discrepancy in the kind of chair that he sat on when he was speaking to Kor, and how this had partially derailed the actual interview since Nathan had to contend with the wholly unprecedented geometry of the real, actual-life chair in Kor's apartment.

The impossible encounter

It is a distinctive feature of the structure of anxiety (and its symptoms of obsession and compulsion) that it moves continually between a catastrophic totality and a fixation on the tiniest of details, a trait we see acted out with both Nathan in *The Rehearsal* and Alan, Nadia's foil in *Russian Doll*. They each obsess over tiny details and seek to pre-control situations. They each defend against the demand of the other to be present – that is, to resist and emote – by seeking instead to placate them. By offering to take care of all their details, both Nathan and Alan spare their others an inconvenience that they are, in fact, craving.

In Alan's case, he has been with Beatrice for nine years, during which time she has felt increasingly suffocated by his endless equivocations and ceaseless worrying. Most infuriating of all is his determination to never do anything 'wrong'. Nadia, when she meets him, is immediately taken aback by his 'perfect posture', which she notes is not something that that either she or her bohemian layabouts are often accused of. We see Alan going through his strict morning routine, putting his body through a regime of weight training and exercises while listening and repeating his positive affirmations. At one point, Nadia erupts with fury when she returns to her apartment to find that Alan has 'tidied up'. He looks on dumbfounded, not able to comprehend how his act of kindness (as he viewed it) was experienced by Nadia as a profound violation of her inner life.

In *The Rehearsal,* we quickly realise that Nathan's business of conducting rehearsals for others is entirely driven by his own need to cast his daily reality into the hypothetical contingency of these elaborately concocted plays. In fact, the show is gradually hijacked by a rehearsal that Nathan has conceived for a woman named Angela, who is thinking of having a child but would like to sample the trials and tribulations of this task first. Nathan rents a house and hires a series of child actors to play a boy they name 'Adam' at three-year intervals, from newborn infancy to the age of eighteen. When the original candidate falls through, Nathan fills in for the role of father, or 'non-romantic co-parent' in the parlance of the situation.

The other rehearsals that Nathan is engaged in thus become framed by this broader rehearsal of family life and his own turn as the *pater familias*. Like Nadia, who finds herself cast into the role of mother in her encounter with Lucy, Nathan finds himself unerringly drawn into the role of father to the various 'Adams' who work their way through the house he is occupying with Angela. Eventually, Nathan and Angela fall out when Nathan asks that Judaism be offered as an alternative religious stance for their 'son'. For Angela, a passive-aggressive Christian fundamentalist, this is a bridge too far and she withdraws from the rehearsal.

At this point, instead of calling the whole thing off, Nathan decides to persist with the rehearsal, with him now in the position of single father. Hence, by degrees, we arrive at the fundamental situation in which Nathan as 'father' confronts himself as 'son' (who is acted out by the child actors who play 'Adam'). The situation, though without the recourse to body-horror, is exactly analogous to the one where Nadia, in the position of 'mother', meets herself as 'daughter' (triggered by her encounter with Lucy).

So it is that in these seemingly quite different programs (*Russian Doll* and *The Rehearsal*) we come to an identical originary moment that instigates the repetition. In both cases, what takes place is a fundamental incommensurability in primary identification: Nathan-as-son cannot be brought into equivalence with Nathan-as-father, just as Nadia-as-daughter cannot be squared with Nadia-as-mother. This impossibility lays bare a fracture at the heart of human subjectivity that becomes visible in the nakedness of their incompatible demands. Both parent and child look to each other with the same demand: look after me. The infantile qualities of both Nadia and Nathan – one wrapped up in a childish cynicism and the other in a childish gullibility – prevent them from occupying the parental signifier, the one that would accept responsibility for the fatality of the situation, even though, in so many ways, it could not be otherwise. It is this failure that causes the repetition, and it is repetition that exists to inscribe the moment of this failure.

Chapter Four

Dissociation

What if, immediately adjacent to the world we live in there was a second world almost identical to this one? This world exists in parallel to ours and shadows us in every way, even to the point that every single living person has their double in this other dimension. This is the premise of *Counterpart* (2017–19), where in 1987 a scientist in East Berlin inadvertently opens a portal to this parallel universe. So, there are two Earths: Earth Alpha, which functions as the primary world, and Earth Prime, which is now connected through a portal in the basement laboratory where the experiment took place. The existence of this second dimension is not disclosed to the general public, but secret diplomatic relations between the two Earths commence. We enter the story 30 years after this momentous event, and in that time a shadowy bureaucracy (the 'Office of Interchange') has emerged, whose task it is to maintain communication with the people of Earth Prime.

The reduplication of the universe that is the premise of *Counterpart* can also be thought of as a split. The very idea of a universe is that it contains everything. But *Counterpart* creates a split in the world and, in this respect, echoes the concept of a 'split diegesis' that was introduced in Chapter 2 in relation to *Homecoming*. The fact that the universe is somehow split – that is to say, that the universe is not universal but conditional – is an intriguing insistence to emerge in the domain of popular culture. The split world also resembles the concept of repetition explored in the previous chapter, except what we have here is not a repetition of a day or an event in time, but of the entirety of existence.

Counterpart

Beneath the shiny exterior of modern office block housing, the Office of Interchange is a dark and dingy tunnel that is the portal between the two universes of Earth Alpha and Earth Prime. This gateway resembles a military checkpoint and is carefully guarded on either side by the most stringent security. While initially harmonious, relations between the two dimensions soured when a deadly flu pandemic swept through Earth Prime, killing millions of people in the early 2000s. Because the same disease did not break out in Earth Alpha, there is a lingering suspicion amongst factions within Earth Prime that the virus was deliberately released by their counterparts in the other dimension to gain a strategic ascendancy.

What we have in *Counterpart* is not just a replication of one world by another (the formal premise of the program), but the replication of the scenario that typified the Cold War era. Between 1945 and 1989, there were in effect two 'worlds', a deadly rivalry between a capitalist 'west' and a communist 'east'. The fact that *Counterpart* is in essence re-enacting a Cold War political thriller, in which the idea of the 'double agent' is literalised, is reinforced by the location of the action in Berlin, which was the archetypal *mise-en-scène* of the Cold War.

Divided Berlin, more than 150 kilometres from the West German border, was itself a reduplication of divided Germany, which was, in turn, the image (or condensation) of a divided Europe. Europe's divisions were echoed in Asia, with splits in Korea and Vietnam, along with bloody and prolonged wars supported by nuclear-armed superpowers. The fundamental contest of the Cold War was not between one world and another, as if it were some abstract lifestyle choice, but something more urgent and exclusive; namely, *what time am I in?* Indeed, the significance of the rivalry between capitalism and socialism is not so much that they represented different worlds – after all, there are many different ways that humans organise themselves across the planet – but that they represented alternative modernities, and it is this dimension, with its uncanny overtones, that *Counterpart* adroitly captures.

Howard and Howard

The heroes of the story are the two Howard Silks. In Earth Alpha, Howard Silk is a mild-mannered, low-level bureaucrat. In characterological terms, this Howard Silk closely resembles Carrasco in the *Homecoming* series, a show that was also styled on the conspiracy thrillers of the Cold War. Both characters are stolid and self-effacing, bullied by their bosses and clinging somewhat pathetically to the rules of the system that cares nothing for them and which they chronically misunderstand. By contrast, the Howard Silk from Earth Prime is a hard-nosed and ruthless political operative, a mixture of the tough-talking hard-boiled detective (the *noir* hero) and the suave spy-hero of espionage thrillers typified by James Bond.

In this way, the entire split between the universes is made to pivot on the vicissitudes of masculinity. The relationship between the worlds is acted out as the relationship between the two Howard Silks, one meek and indignant, and the other tough and belligerent. At the sexual level, the first Howard dotes selflessly on his wife, who is in a coma following a car accident. Unbeknownst to him, his wife is a high-level agent in the Office of Interchange and having an affair with another man. The second Howard treats women warily, which is to say he treats them with a good deal more respect, and grants them far greater agency, than the mollycoddling first Howard.

What we see in the split between the two Howards is that the two worlds are not differentiated by technology or ideology but on a relationship of knowledge. The first Howard Silk is a dupe and a stooge, while the second Howard Silk has seen it all before and is aware of how things run on both sides of the divide. Yet, when stripped of its performative masculinity, things take on a different complexion. Indeed, one could say that, in many ways, the first Howard Silk is actually the beneficiary of all the work that the second Howard Silk does 'behind the scenes'. The first Howard Silk has lived a comfortable life of carefully maintained ignorance, while the second Howard Silk has fought tooth and nail to uphold the interests of his masters.

Fight Club

We also see the show takes the form of a kind of education, and in this respect is a variant of the belated *bildungsroman* that underpinned the time loop narratives in the previous chapter. In this new scenario, rather than a loop in time, it is the figure of the double (*doppelgänger*) that arrives unexpectedly to fracture the 'innocence' of the adult character trapped in a persistent infancy. The most prominent recent example of the device of the double, at least insofar as it is used to work through the dynamics of masculine maturity, is David Fincher's influential film *Fight Club* (1999), adapted from Chuck Palahniuk's 1996 novel. *Fight Club* is a modern variant of the *doppelgänger* story that was prominent in key literary works of the nineteenth century, including Poe's story 'William Wilson' (1839), Dostoyevsky's novella *The Double* (1846), Stevenson's *The Strange Case of Dr Jekyll and Mr Hyde* (1886) and Wilde's *The Picture of Dorian Gray* (1890). In all of these texts there is this contrast between masculine duty (depicted as meekness) and masculine will (depicted as obscene pleasure). The mediated possibilities of cinema afforded some advantages in the depiction of this theme, since the same actor could play both figures, even in the same scene, and there is a rich tradition of *doppelgänger* movies in cinematic history.

In *Fight Club*, the meek unnamed narrator (played by Edward Norton) finds his life turned upside down by the arrival of the charismatic Tyler Durden (played by Brad Pitt). Tyler's reckless iconoclasm and casual disregard for the norms of society both offends and excites the narrator. Tyler chastises the narrator for his soulless conformism and challenges him to claim what is his in the world. At the heart of the narrator's transformation (that is, his *bildung* or education) from empty salaryman to macho world-beater is a secret society where men fight each other consensually with their bare fists. This activity is eroticised insofar as both combatants 'enjoy' the activity and the result of the fight is largely irrelevant. The erotic terms of this encounter are sadomasochistic and revolve around the pleasure of seeing injuries marked out on their bodies. In effect, these men sign each other's bodies. The next day, these same people exchange knowing glances on the subway or in the supermarket, where their black eyes and split lips are the sign of their secret homosocial bond.

At the conclusion of *Fight Club* there is a big reveal, wherein we learn that, all along, Tyler Durden was none other than the narrator himself, a dissociated alter ego. Tyler was a figure that actualised, as the *expression* of his masculinity, every element that the narrator renounced as the *price* of masculinity. In psychoanalytic terms, Tyler is a fantasy figure that springs into existence to give shape to the reality of castration, which is the psychic understanding of the renunciation of violence (including sexual violence) that is the core of our inscription as subjects in the world. In this way, castration (foundational renunciation) is the universal price of becoming legal subjects. To obtain our symbolic existence, to occupy a place within language and social reality, we are castrated into the symbolic order. *Fight Club* gives expression to this operation by acting out a compensatory fantasy.

Masculine anxiety

At this point, we notice a certain ambiguity, because on the one hand, we have stories that involve the appearance of a *doppelgänger,* and on the other, we have the more wide-ranging device of a parallel universe, in which not just a particular person, but the entirety of existence is doubled. In some ways, this distinction resembles the one that separates the amnesia plot from the time loop story. In the amnesia plot the hero loses their memory, and the story is about them recovering it. The time loop story reverses this: the hero keeps their memory, but the rest of the world is amnesiac, starting each new day with no recollection that it has already happened. A similar symmetry is visible when comparing the *doppelgänger* story to the parallel universe story. The key element in each story is haunting. In the *doppelgänger* story, the hero is haunted by their double. In the parallel universe story, the hero is not haunted by their double. Instead, the hero intercedes – often in concert with their double – to restore the veil that prevents the world from knowing that it is haunted by a second world.

In *Counterpart* there is also an ambiguity about what is causing the doubling. At the political level, the parallel universes, each mutually suspicious of the other, seem to be a literalisation of geopolitical rivalry, where nations or blocs compete against each other for strategic supremacy. But, at the personal level, we have this anxious division of masculinity acted out between the two Howard Silks, and split into abject meekness and Nietzschean machismo. The simple synthesis would be to say that global political rivalry is the expression at the collective level of the masculine will to power that exists at the personal level. Certainly, the recent return of the 'strong man' leader (authoritarian saviour) in leading world powers gives support to the essential congruity of everyday masculine competitiveness with contests at the geopolitical level.

Counterpart is clearly centred on the contests of masculinity. Indeed, when asked why the critically acclaimed show was not renewed for a third season, the streaming

service (Starz) explained: 'Counterpart was a great show …
but it was a very complicated show, a very male show. We had
picked that show up and made a two-season commitment
before we'd honed in on this premium female strategy.' Yet,
what if each of these levels, the intimate level of masculine
anxiety and the geopolitical level of strategic supremacy,
were the expression of something more profound? What
if what the show is trying to grasp is not how men beating
their chests is the cause of war and endless competition, but
some primal discord that instigates a structural insecurity at
the subjective level?

Severance

Let us now turn to a different example of a show premised
on a parallel universe. In *Severance* (2022–), a biotechnology
company called Lumon has developed a medical procedure
(severance) that partitions memories and experiences. The
procedure offers a radical solution to what is called, in
contemporary human resources parlance, the problem of
'work-life balance'. Rather than daydreaming at work about
everything other than work, and then going home and not
being able to stop thinking about work, severance creates a
wall of amnesia (repression) between these two dimensions.

Lumon employees who have elected to have the
procedure drive to work in the morning, park their car in
the sprawling staff carpark, say hello to the concierge and
walk on through to the elevator. However, the elevator
is not actually an elevator, but a portal, and when the
employee exits from it, they have been silently shorn of their
underlying memories and is now free to work unencumbered
by any outside ties and worries. The ontological status of

this workspace remains ambiguous and might be thought of as a kind of 'metaverse', even though the people are inhabiting the same body that they inhabit on the outside.

During their working day, these employees work in teams on abstract tasks. We follow the characters in the Macrodata Refinement Department whose work consists of watching numbers swirl on their oddly old-fashioned computer screens, and removing the aberrant numbers. These workers know how to complete their task, but have no sense of what its purpose might be. Indeed, they show a distinct lack of curiosity, as if questions like this belong firmly in the province of life's imponderables or are guarded by a silent taboo.

In this respect, the severed workers of Lumon are, in Marxist terms, ideal practitioners of alienated labour. They labour serenely at jobs they neither understand nor especially care to. They seem unaffected by the anxiety and boredom that is the inevitable by-product of alienated work and so, while they are formally and purely alienated from their tasks, they do not suffer from a sense of alienation. This is the miraculous achievement of the severance procedure. At the end of their allotted time, they descend in the elevator and the procedure is reversed. All recollection of their working day is locked away, and the memories of their outside life seamlessly reappear. They get back in their cars and drive home.

Who are you?

The show begins in disquieting fashion with a woman neatly dressed, but unconscious and sprawled in an ungainly fashion on a long table in an empty, brightly lit boardroom. As she wakes, a voice addresses her insistently from a speaker in the room, repeating the question, 'Who are you?' The bewildered woman does not answer and searches frantically for an exit, but the door is locked. In a more conciliatory tone, the voice asks the woman if she would mind taking a short survey. Eventually, with no real alternative, she agrees and the survey is conducted in the semi-automated fashion of telephone surveys, where one has the uncanny feeling that one is speaking to a person who is also at the same time a computer.

The first question asks the woman to give her name. With a look of painful confusion, she realises that she does not know. The final question asks her to say the colour of her mother's eyes – again, she cannot. Wracked by a terrifying uncertainty, the woman hears the voice congratulate her for getting 'a perfect score'. A man then enters the room and introduces himself as Mark, and explains to her that her name is Helly. He explains that her outside self, known colloquially as her 'outie', has elected to undergo severance. She is then brought through to meet the rest of Mark's team in the Macrodata Refinement Department.

What we have depicted here is a reconstitution of the foundational moment of symbolic birth. In the discussion of *Counterpart*, the concept of castration was introduced to account for the appearance of an uncanny übermensch, a second Howard Silk who has all the elements of potency that the first Howard Silk seemed to lack. In *Severance*, we open with what is, in effect, a dramatisation of this foundational moment of castration. What transpires in the 'interview' between the voice and Helly is a decision without a choice. In the first instance, there is only one door, and it is locked from the outside. Moreover, there is only one voice, and the voice knows. The subject knows nothing – not her name, not even the colour of her mother's eyes.

Helly is given a clipped version of her backstory. She is also given an occupation, although its purpose remains opaque, and the slightly stilted companionship of her fellow workers. This is what it means to say that the subject is castrated into the symbolic order. Of course, the concept of castration references the removal of the sexual organ, but in *Severance* what is severed is the memory of who one is on the 'outside'. If we credit this equivalence, what we might also venture is that the amnesia plot is one that has emerged to express the foundational reality of castration, a concept which must be understood not in terms of the organ itself, but everything that it represents at the level of action and identity.

Dramatic irony

In *Severance*, we see a number of the features that have characterised the conceptual programs we have considered thus far. In the first place, we have a version of the amnesia plot – with a beautiful young woman waking up having forgotten who she is. Then we have the *mise-en-scène* of the faceless bureaucratic corporation styled in discreet minimalism and filled with faux empathy, just as in the Homecoming Transition Support Centre from *Homecoming* and the Office of Interchange in *Counterpart*. We also have that essential paranoid structure where the other has an other. When we follow Mark home, for instance, he speaks to his neighbour, the kindly bumbling Mrs Selvig, whose nosiness and presumption is tolerated by Mark as an overflow of maternal exuberance. But we experience a shock of recognition, as Mrs Selvig is, in fact, Ms Cobel, Mark's icy, waspish boss on the 'inside'. So, the other – his seemingly innocent neighbour Mrs Selvig – has an other (Ms Cobel), the true master of the whole situation and the hidden face of the Lumon corporation.

Here we can also see the close relationship that the paranoid structure has to the literary phenomenon known as dramatic irony. In dramatic irony, the audience knows things the characters do not, so that when they make assumptions about a state of affairs, we feel a sense of pity or, sometimes, glee at their ignorance. In this show, it is the severance procedure that creates the structural conditions for dramatic irony. But, more generally, this is a useful reminder that wherever we encounter dramatic irony, we should also ask what has been severed; that is, where in this fictional structure is the line that splits the subject?

The show's bifurcation of the world into an 'inside' and 'outside' is intriguing, not least because the allocation of inner and outer realities goes against expectation. We tend to think of our working selves as our 'outer' personality, something we perform on the stage of social reality. We conceptualise our inner life as something more authentic, a core of feelings, memories and intimate relationships that constitute our true self. But in *Severance,* the vantage point is primarily from those who think of themselves as the 'innies', namely those who are working in the Macrodata Refinement Department. In other words, in *Severance,* the outer world of work lays claim to inner reality.

Indeed, Ben Stiller, who produced and directed the show was initially attracted to the script because it was an ingenious refiguring of the office comedy. The main action is between the oddball characters in this office space, who have nothing in common except a job that they do not understand. But it turns out that, in another way, this means they have everything in common. This is the strange dimension of social life in the capitalist era. On the one hand, capitalism atomises human society into individuals and small nuclear families, annihilating the clannish bonds of extended families that hoard their resources internally and prevent the free flow of consumption. On the other hand, capitalism throws people together in workplaces who have nothing to bond them except the instrumental aims of production or service and the endless striving for efficiency.

Public and private

Thus, we have the now conventional split between public (work) and private (family) lives. In office comedies, however, a certain reversal is dramatised. In office comedies, including seminal works like the film *Office Space* (1999) or Ricky Gervais's *The Office* (2001–03) and its long-running

Severance courtesy of Alamy.

US successor (2005–13), one slowly gathers the impression that the office is the true site of these characters' lives, even when their work is utterly meaningless, and that outside this is the nagging loneliness of life in the small, segregated homes of contemporary urban existence. The office comedy, by making the work meaningless and abject, strips away the cloak of purposefulness that dignifies the work in, say, legal or medical dramas. In this respect, we can see that the office comedy has a parallel with prison dramas, such as *Orange is the New Black*. In prison dramas, we have a formalisation of the 'inside' and in *Orange is the New Black,* it is made abundantly clear that the life of almost every character, including the guards, is substantially better inside the prison than it is on the outside.

A typical episode of *Orange is the New Black* consists of a dual storyline centred on one of the female prisoners. An incident in the prison will strike them, and at the same time the show will 'flash back' to a corresponding moment in their pre-prison life. The episode will then alternate between the situation in the prison (conceptualised as 'inside') and their former life on the outside. By the end of the episode, it is painfully obvious that the world outside is infinitely crueller and more perverse that the inside world of prison life, despite its overt forms of coercion. The crucial differentiation, in fact, is the functional sociality of prison life, its quasi-military collectivist ethos. Certainly, we know that the show is, in some ways, an idealisation of incarceration, but on the other hand, we see that the reality of non-carceral life for these women, who are on the whole poor and marginalised, can easily reach a point whereby prison presents as a genuine social alternative.

What is more important than whether *Orange is the New Black* is an accurate rendering of prison life is that the drama is structurally dependent on this split between an inside and outside. In using a dual storyline connected by flashbacks, the show follows a narrative pattern pioneered in the serial *Lost* (2004–10). In *Lost*, an airliner crashes on a mysterious island in the Pacific and, as the survivors try to make a life for themselves, the show flashes back to their earlier lives. The flashbacks are connected to the present moment by a traumatic hinge, such that a troubling incident on the island immediately casts the character back to a parallel moment in their earlier life.

It is never made clear whether these earlier moments in *Lost* are being consciously recollected by the character or are simply presented to us, the audience, under the guise of dramatic irony. This ambiguity is crucial to *Lost* and also *Orange is the New Black* because it opens up the possibility that these earlier events are unconscious, and in this respect, the show introduces the unconscious as such. It is significant that what introduces the unconscious is repetition. The two events, the one in the notional present (the prison, the island) and the one in the past of the flashback (the life outside, the life before) are joined because they enact an essential moment, a moment when the subject is put into question. The fact that two moments repeat raises the further prospect that these are not the only repetitions, but part of a compulsively repeating series, which is the scenario we encounter in the time loop stories.

Inside and outside

As well as the quality of parallelism that prison dramas and office comedies introduce, the other major feature is this inversion of inside and outside. Of the office workers in *Severance*, it is only Mark that we see both inside (in the workplace) and outside, living alone in his small, neat row house. Mark's lonely existence outside of work contrasts strongly with the chirpy banter of his workplace. In an early scene, we see him weeping uncontrollably in the carpark before work. He eventually gathers himself together, dries his eyes and trudges into the building.

In a locker room, he deposits his winter coat and boots, along with his wallet and car keys, before proceeding through the elevator that will take him to the 'severed' floor of the Lumon building, and at the same time trigger the chip implanted in his brain to switch him over to his work self. In the elevator, a close-up on Mark's face shows the almost imperceptible moment when his face loses its melancholic cast and is replaced with that characteristic office cheerfulness, which is the accepted demeanour of the workplace. The extradiegetic music changes key and tempo as well. Leaving the elevator with a bounce in his step that was utterly missing when he walked into work, Mark is briefly perplexed by the presence of the wet tissue in his pocket, the legacy of his earlier misery. He shrugs his shoulders, throws it in the bin, and saunters off down the corridor.

What is interesting in the case of *Severance* is there is not any duplicity in the basic set-up. The people on the 'outside' are not kidnapped or surreptitiously apprehended, but voluntarily submit to the severance procedure. Each day they go to their jobs at Lumon in the full knowledge that they will remember nothing between the time they enter the magical elevator and exit it eight hours later. In other words, they fully know that they do not know, if we can put it this way. Likewise, their selves on the 'inside' are made aware of their situation once they enter, as we see in the case of Helly on her first day.

Once inside, these newly minted workers retain their memories from their time there, and carry on conversations with their fellow workers ensconced in this universe. Everyone is aware that they have outies who live their lives oblivious to this workaday universe, and they trust that this is a decision they have made in their wisdom and for the sake of their well-being. The innies maintain, by and large, a kindly sense of kinship to their outies, although they do confess to a degree of curiosity about what they might get up to on the outside. The relationship resembles the shy curiosity that students feel towards their teachers, who they know have 'outside' lives that are not quite commensurable with their roles inside the institution of learning.

The suffering subject

And yet, despite this seemingly perfect separation of work from life, the tension in the program comes from the emergence of signs that disrupt the purity of this division. In other words, symptoms emerge. A symptom is a compromise formation that attempts to service competing imperatives. Helly is, herself, one of the key places that symptoms emerge. With her, the procedure seems to not quite have worked in the way that it should have. She does not seem to be properly insulated by the bubble of equanimity that encases Mark and the others in the Macrodata Refinement Department.

Perhaps it is early days, and the procedure takes a while to settle in, but Helly shows little sign of becoming the docile worker drone that is meant to be the outcome of severance. She reacts violently to her incarceration and continually plots her escape. She refuses Mark's overtures of workplace confraternity and regards everyone in the workplace, no matter how outwardly kind, as her enemy. Because she tries to smuggle a message to her outie alerting her to the terror of life inside, Helly is subjected to a corrective punishment. This is administered in a specially constructed cell and involves her having to repeat again and again a mantra of obedience. After this, she takes the radical step of attempting suicide by hanging herself in the elevator. She is saved by the security staff, and they show her a video made by her outie explaining that she has no intention of reversing the severance procedure. Helly realises she has been outflanked by her own self.

What is happening here? The situation can be clarified if we follow the suffering subject. In Mark's case, we have severance as it is meant to work. Outside he is deeply depressed and downcast. At a dinner with his sister and her husband, we learn that Mark was once a history professor, but when his wife died, he was overcome by grief and his life fell apart. He resigned his position at the university and signed up for a job as a severed worker at Lumon. The impetus for Mark's decision, in other words, was to have at least part of each day free of the suffering caused by the loss of his wife. And this does seem to occur, with a noticeable change in Mark's mood when he is 'inside'.

Mark's improved mood is fairly subtle and does not descend into the blithering cheerfulness of Jim Carrey's character in *The Truman Show* (1998). He retains a certain grudging quality that comes over as quizzical circumspection and wry humour. And there is also a lingering sadness in his eyes, which the elevator cannot quite remediate. Nevertheless, in Mark's case, what we appear to have is him suffering on the outside and not suffering on the inside. What the show gets us to understand though, is that there is something ineffably sadder about the Mark on the inside. Inside Mark is suffering through the absence of suffering. Because he cannot suffer like the outside Mark who weeps in his car every morning, inside Mark's life takes on a grotesque provisional quality. The pitiable, but ultimately very human, question for outside Mark is why must I suffer? For inside Mark, there is the far more destabilising question: where has my suffering gone?

If we look at Helly, we see that this situation has become inverted, or at least compromised by a fatal bleeding through. Inside Helly clearly continues to suffer. Her bewilderment does not retreat, as it does for her fellow innies, behind a wall of equanimity. She feels an existential agony, sensing some unbearable impossibility. But, like those caught in time loops, she cannot escape – as it was for Nadia and Alan in *Russian Doll* (and Phil in *Groundhog Day*), even suicide is foreclosed. She must continue to live on and on in a repetitive, empty fashion. Meanwhile, the video that outside Helly sends her innie, reveals a callous certainty in her decision to undergo severance and her determination to keep the situation exactly as it is. Helly, who had thought her outie would act to end her nightmare once she was made aware of its true horror, is instead confronted with the shocking revelation that this state of affairs is exactly as she (outside Helly) wants it.

Political action

While Helly experiences the pain of defeat, outflanked by her own self, she also precipitates political action. Helly's arrival in the Macrodata Refinement Team introduces the very thing that was missing from their world: actual suffering.

At first, they attempt to correct this, trying to either cheer her up or suggest that her feelings are best forgotten; and really, this is not such a bad place; in fact, we have quite a bit of fun, etc. But, as time passes and Helly's suffering remains both intractable and insistent, the gradual effect is that, one by one, her fellow innies themselves begin to suffer. This is an example of hystericisation, and suggests how the suffering subject (bleeding heart) is the origin of political movement.

The situation is reminiscent of the role of Offred in *The Handmaid's Tale*. Like Helly, Offred refuses to either accept the determinations of the world she has been cast into or make the compromises necessary to cope with it. What *Severance* does, though, is decline the theatrical devices offered by the contemporary dystopian imaginary. The world in which we suffer is not awaiting us in the dystopian future; it's the very one we live in right here and right now. Within contemporary capitalist modernity, the human subject has signed away something vital in the very moment they accepted the division that is demanded to simply live within its precepts. What *Severance* exposes is the sacrifice demanded by capitalist realism as the price of its reality – a reality driven by a law of efficiency that acknowledges no human limit. The radical act in this system is to become the living emblem of this limit, which is the role given to Helly in the series. It is by being this living limit that she disrupts the 'inner' workings of everyday life.

The Upside Down

We can see refractions of each of the four concepts touched upon in this book (amnesia, repetition, dissociation, dystopia) in one of the defining shows of the streaming era, the flagship Netflix drama *Stranger Things* (2016–). In this show, set in a lovingly stylised version of 1980s suburban America, a group of boys who have bonded over their love of the Dungeons and Dragons role-playing game discover the existence of an alternative plane of existence. Nearby, in a secret government facility (cf. *Homecoming, Counterpart*), a covert science experiment is taking place that is giving children strange and terrifying new powers the military is seeking to harness. One night, one of the boys, Will Byers, is abducted by a supernatural creature and, at the same time, a child from the government facility, known only by her number 'Eleven', escapes and finds refuge in the home of one of the boys.

When the boys ask Eleven where she has come from, they realise she cannot or will not speak, and she only communicates through gestures and facial expressions. Pressed on her origins, Eleven levitates the Dungeons and Dragons board into the air and points to its blank underside. The boys immediately understand that Eleven has come from 'The Upside Down', a realm that is welded directly onto ours, but only visible through certain uncanny inconsistencies that intrude on the common-sense world. This is coded into the world of the film via the conventions of horror cinema, with lights flickering, walls distending, and spooky monsters lurking in the background. Adding to this is the fact that only children and the slightly deranged can 'see' these phenomena, and that the parents of the children remain blind to the goings on, explaining them away with maddening ease. It is only the social misfits (the boys) who can see the persistence of elements that are excluded from official reality.

The narrative is instigated by an exchange of beings: as Will is captured by The Upside Down, Eleven emerges into daily reality, albeit under the cover of the boys' care. The element of amnesia is sustained by Eleven, who can only patchily remember the horrors of the experiments that were performed on her by the sinister doctor that she calls 'Papa'. The mark of repetition is caught in the fact of the exchange: one suffering child (Eleven) can only be released on the condition that another is held hostage (Will). One might say that The Upside Down demands its pound of flesh, but the show introduces a fundamental moral ambiguity whereby The Upside Down is also, despite its monstrous decay and terrifying darkness, the site of a certain life-affirming truth. In that sense, we might equally say that capitalist realism demands its pound of flesh, and The Upside Down is the true locality of the living being.

It is useful to compare the divided world of *Stranger Things* with the divided worlds we saw in *Counterpart* and *Severance*. On the face of it they seem rather different. In *Counterpart*, the two worlds are *almost* identical. Rather than a contrast between conventional sleepy reality and a horrifying realm of monsters, the difference between the two Earths in *Counterpart* is mainly visible at the seemingly banal level of character. A similar pattern was visible in *Severance*, wherein the personality shift that takes place between a character's innie and outie is the key signal that we are in different places.

A way to explain this contrast between the divided world in *Stranger Things*, where the shadow world is a monstrous and baroque hellscape, and the ones in *Counterpart* and *Severance*, which are marked by slight, uncanny differences, is to say that the latter situation (subtle difference) is the result of the repression of the former situation (radical difference). The secular modernity of capitalist realism and scientific rationality is premised on the strict circumscription of reality. It presumes to have no true limit to the knowability of its world, but certain things remain stubbornly inexplicable,

Stranger Things courtesy of Netflix.

not least the proliferation of what are regarded as mental illnesses. Will capitalism ever cure suicide? What would this mean?

Thus, just as we did with the fallen worlds of dystopian narratives, we can also regard the horror at the centre of *Stranger Things* as perversely utopian. The boys and those who join them, a collection of misfits and outcasts, find themselves revitalised by their engagement with The Upside Down. It is this realm that saves the small town from its zombie-like somnolence, animating a dull suburbia of quiet misery with cosmological significance and inscribing an ethic of justice based on rescuing the child from the grip of our instrumental demands.

Symptoms of the digital age

What, then, of the other argument that this book has attempted, which is that conceptual television is symptomatic of the digital age? And, the more specific contention that streamed content constitutes a rupture with the preceding paradigms of cinema, broadcast television, and tape and disc recordings (such as DVD box sets)? It must be said that this is the more tenuous claim. The evidence suggests not so much a step change as a more subtle emergence of accents and emphases. Hopefully, this book lays some groundwork for the further investigation of this relationship.

In the proliferation of dystopian narratives traced in Chapter One, we noted that the premise antedates the emergence of streamed drama. Nevertheless, dystopian stories have become, in many ways, the distinctive plot of the contemporary age, giving expression to fears of scientific overreach, political totalitarianism and environmental collapse. The cultural prominence of dystopian fictions has taken hold, even though we hardly need to invent such worlds, given what is taking place in the domain of reality. Indeed, the 'what if' of the dystopian premise seems, in many cases, to be on the verge of redundancy. It is as though the hyperbole of fiction is only introduced in order to reassure us that the actual reality we inhabit is not quite as bad as it could be.

Still, against the conventional view that dystopia is expressive of contemporary fears and anxieties that are related to very real phenomena and trends, I placed a second proposition that dystopian narratives often delivered utopian outcomes. Notably, there was the revitalisation of life, especially gendered life, in survivor epics such as *The Walking Dead*, and now very much visible in the HBO zombie series *The Last of Us* (2023–) Moreover, it was argued that dystopian narrative is the cultural mode that has evolved to challenge the hegemony of capitalist realism. In the contrasting examples of *The Handmaid's Tale* and *Squid Game*, what came strongly into view was the figure of the master. Again, we could see in both these stories a revivifying project, where it was the master – spectralised and alienated as the invisible hand of the market in modern capitalism – who takes on a bold new form and, despite his impotence, demands direct pleasure from his slaves. The dystopian story is animated by the demand to please the master. It is only in the face of that implacable demand that the hero can come to fruition.

In the case of memory in Chapter Two, we saw how the digital era has witnessed the re-emergence of the amnesia plot, so popular in the cinema of the 1940s. I suggested that the contemporary sense of memory is now inevitably inflected by the idea of data storage we experience through our interfaces with digital devices. Particularly revealing was the collision we saw in *I May Destroy You* between the amnesia plot and the *bildungsroman*. In that show, the amnesia plot migrated from its origins in cinematic crime and thriller genres into the formation story of a young adult. What this indicated was a failure of developmental education (*bildung*) and, in its place, a traumatic hole in experience that became the fulcrum of maturation. The implication is that there has been an alienation of memory as such, as if the foundational memories of subjective life are now subject to the kinds of data manipulation that are available in our devices. This helps account for the films and shows that feature either the direct removal of a memory (*Eternal Sunshine of the Spotless Mind, Homecoming*) or their calculated insertion (*Blade Runner* [1982], *Inception* [2010]).

There is a sharper picture in the case of repetition in Chapter Three. The time loop story is not one that is much in evidence before the 1980s, which is the era when it became possible, via the availability of video cassettes, to re-watch movies and shows at will. But the premise really accelerates in the digital era, with DVDs and streamed content. What stands out is how, just as in the amnesia plot, the repetition plot takes on the educative role once reserved for the *bildungsroman*. Indeed, we saw that in the examples we considered (*Groundhog Day*, *Russian Doll*, *The Rehearsal*), the day (or event) is repeated with the clear goal of achieving a mature acceptance of one's situation. Put simply, the time loop is the mechanism for a belated growing up. The salient element is perhaps the quality of belatedness, which seems to take on a universal quality in the contemporary moment. Insofar as the time loop is structured towards sentimental education, TV is staying true – even in the streaming era – to its traditional pedagogical role, in which it instructs its citizens in the skills of daily living.

The relationship that repetition has to the digital age must remain speculative, but what it does seem to suggest is that there is something lost now that we have everything directly to hand. The fact that all knowledge, and even a multitudinous array of services and products, are just sitting there waiting for us to access them has caused a crisis in education. There is a new paradox in which we apparently know everything, or could if we simply clicked the right button, but at the same time, remain utterly clueless. This cluelessness is what gets exposed in the time loop story. In the time loop story, repetition intercedes to remind us that there is something very important that we do not know, and that the only way to know it is to act it out in the domain of the other.

There is also a symptomatic resemblance between our lives now, divided between online and offline domains, and the concept we encountered in Chapter Four, which involved the splitting of worlds and the dissociation of selves. Yet, here we can also see a reversal of the sociological causality we tend to invoke for changes in the way we live. I have, for instance, suggested that changes in the material delivery of dramatic narratives (such as the emergence of streamed television) effect changes in the form of those narratives. The emergence of digital devices has certainly changed the way we live, and it is widely understood to have had psychological consequences, such as lessening our attention span or making us less able to deal with real life social complexity and the reality of emotions. In this scheme, we understand the device to be the cause. But what if something in our psychic life has, in fact, demanded the device be created? After all, the device did not invent itself.

In both *Counterpart* and *Severance*, we watch as beings contend with the shadowy existence of their own other. The emergence of such stories parallels the emergence of our capacity to conduct ourselves in the world split across the alternative fields of online and offline life. Doesn't the second Howard Silk, the aggressive go-getter who compensates for the browbeaten first Howard Silk, exactly correspond to the classic genesis of the internet troll? What *Severance* captures is the powerful ambivalence that attaches to this solution. *Severance* shows that the split in the subject, which allows the human to meet radically competing demands, also causes a hollowing out in the respective avatars. They become haunted by the hole in themselves, which is the principal sign of their divided state.

It will be noticed that one of the themes of this book has been education. In many ways, if we think about the tribulations depicted in conceptual television – dystopia, amnesia, repetition, dissociation – we encounter the affective signatures of our schooling. This is another way in which conceptual television should be understood as fundamentally pedagogical.

But why do we need our streamed shows to school us when we have schools that do this job? The answer lies in the way that growing up, in so many of these programs, was seen to falter. This arrested maturity manifested as a breakdown in the efficacy of the education narrative (the *bildungsroman*). The problem was not that information was being withheld, but that the mechanism for incorporating it was missing. Conceptual television gives shape to this missing element through the typology of its plots.

We can thus see conceptual television as a curious form of rescue. Against the illusion, fostered by the internet (and now AI), that everything is already known and to hand, conceptual television asserts as a founding premise that knowledge sits in a place beyond us. Indeed, conceptual television is a restoration of the subject in the freedom of their humiliation. Despite their embarrassment, the hero in these programs finds themselves viscerally released from the constant pretence that they already know everything.

Chapter Notes and Further Reading

Introduction

Television studies is a lively field. In a scholarly sense, television was first treated seriously by the British New Left and, in many ways, television studies has evolved along with the broader study of mass culture. My own grounding in the field draws on the seminal comparative media theory of Marshall McLuhan, particularly his classic study *Understanding Media* (Routledge and Kegan Paul, 1964). A more recent intervention was Lev Manovich's brilliant *The Language of New Media* (MIT Press, 2001), which offered a searching phenomenology of digital media, locating it against earlier forms and introducing the concept of 'the interface'. Manovich's book also offers, in my view, the sharpest theorisation of the screen as it occurs in modern life. Jay Bolter and Richard Grusin's book *Remediation: Understanding New Media* (MIT Press, 1999) has also been influential for me and others in seeking to understand the desire of the user in relation to new media. In other words, is it our seeking immersion in media's virtual space, or something else? There are also some excellent works of media studies that come from sociology, most notably John Thompson's ground-breaking *The Media and Modernity* (Stanford University Press, 1995). Drawing on Thompson's work, Shaun Moores' *Media/Theory: Thinking About Media and Communications* (Routledge, 2005) introduced me to the concept of 'cyclicity' as a means to think about television's various cycles.

In terms of the emergent critical literature on streamed television, there have been important contributions by established television scholars such as in Amanda D. Lotz's *Portals: A Treatise on Internet-Distributed Television* (Michigan Publishing Services, 2017) and the second edition of Lotz and Jonathan Gray's *Television Studies* (Polity Press, 2019), which begins with an introduction titled 'Still Television Studies?' Ramon Lobato's *Netflix Nations: The Geography of Digital Distribution* (NYU Press, 2019) and MJ Robinson's *Television on Demand: Curatorial Culture and the Transformation of TV* (Bloomsbury Academic, 2017) have cast a useful light on the new material conditions that are determining streamed content. However, I have been most influenced by two excellent studies of the form of contemporary television: Jason Mittell's *Complex TV: The Poetics of Contemporary Television Storytelling* (NYU Press, 2015) and JP Kelly's *Time, Technology and Narrative Form in Contemporary US Television Drama: Pause, Rewind, Record* (Springer, 2017). While not restricting themselves to streamed content, both Mittell and Kelly offer powerful assessments of changes in the poetics of televisual drama.

At a more fundamental level, in terms of how I conceive key relationships between media, the psyche and social reality, I am indebted to the psychoanalytic study of culture, and most particularly to Lacanian film studies. Here, my guiding lights have been the works of Slavoj Žižek, Joan

Copjec, Alenka Zupančič, Todd McGowan and Mark Fisher, and I cite them in more detail later. Ryan Engley's excellent essay 'Psychoanalytic Seriality as Media Theory: From Freud's Couch to Yours' in *Continental Thought & Theory* (vol. 3, no. 2, 2021)is the best application of Lacanian theory to social television.

Chapter One: Dystopia

This chapter begins by invoking the concept of 'capitalist realism', which is one that I return to at regular points in the book. The term was proposed by Mark Fisher in his book *Capitalist Realism: Is There No Alternative?* (Zero Books, 2019). This is a short but rich account of the problem that capitalism poses for any meaningful resistance or alternative. Fisher is also a perceptive cultural critic, with often brilliant readings of films exemplifying his analyses. If you have a bit more time on your hands, then Fredric Jameson's *Archaeologies of the Future: The Desire Called Utopia and Other Science Fictions* (Verso, 2005) is a magisterial analysis of utopian and dystopian writing that stretches from contemporary speculative fiction to Thomas More.

When I treat *The Handmaid's Tale* as 'melodrama', I am drawing heavily on Laura Mulvey's brilliant analysis of Douglas Sirk's Hollywood melodramas of the 1950s. Particularly useful are the essays 'Notes on Sirk and Melodrama' from her book *Visual and Other Pleasures* (Palgrave, 1989) and 'Social Hieroglyphics: Reflections on Two Films by Douglas Sirk' from her later book *Fetishism and Curiosity* (Indiana University Press, 1996). An excellent contemporary scholar of screen melodrama is Monique Rooney, and her book *Living Screens: Melodrama and Plasticity in Contemporary Film and Television* (Rowman and Littlefield, 2015) is very helpful in showing the continued functioning of this modality.

I touch briefly on reality television in this chapter, inasmuch as it constitutes the formal backdrop to fictional texts like *The Hunger Games* and *Squid Game*. There is some good scholarship on reality television, including important books – all called *Reality TV* – by Annette Hill (Routledge, 2015), June Deery (Polity Press, 2015) and Jon Kraszewski (Taylor and Francis, 2017). I can also highly recommend Misha Kavka's essay 'Reality TV: Its Contents and Discontents' in in *Critical Quarterly* (vol. 60, no. 4, 2018: 5–18).

In talking about *The Walking Dead*, I draw a distinction between use and exchange value. This is a classical Marxist classification, and a lucid contemporary account of Marxist concepts can be found in David Harvey's *Seventeen Contradictions and the End of Capitalism* (Oxford University Press, 2014). My thinking around zombies has been influenced by a fine short book on the subject by Jennifer Rutherford simply called *Zombies* (Routledge, 2013).

My invocation of the master-slave dialectic to account for the kind of dystopian texts that feature particular forms of abjection and domination (such as *The Handmaid's Tale* and *Squid Game*) comes from my reading of Hegel's *Phenomenology of the Spirit* (1807). If anyone has tried reading Hegel – congratulations, it is no easy task. Fortunately, some of the most important thinkers of recent times have also devoted time to explicating Hegel's foundational writing. Despite his notorious iconoclasm, Slavoj Žižek is one of the best contemporary commentators on Hegel, and *Reading Hegel* (Polity, 2021), by Slavoj Žižek, Frank Ruda and Agon Hamza, is a good place to start, as is Fredric Jameson's *The*

Hegel Variations: On the Phenomenology of Spirit (Verso, 2010). Žižek's book *Tarrying with the Negative: Kant, Hegel and the Critique of Ideology* (Duke University Press Books, 1993) is still a classic and offers a powerful synthesis of dialectical philosophy and psychoanalysis.

Chapter Two: Amnesia

The concern for memory in this chapter links this book to the large field of memory studies, and also to the more specialised field that considers the role of media in shaping social memory. Key books include Peter Rollins and Gary Edgerton's *Television Histories: Shaping Collective Memory in the Media Age* (University Press of Kentucky, 2001); *On Media Memory: Collective Memory in a New Media Age* (Palgrave, 2011), edited by Motti Neiger, Oren Meyers, and Eyal Zandberg; and Joanne Garde-Hansen's *Media and Memory* (Edinburgh University Press, 2011). There are also useful discussions of memory in Andrew Murphie and John Potts' book *Culture and Technology* (Palgrave, 2003). On the particular subject of the amnesia plot in classical Hollywood, I cite David Bordwell's essay, 'The Amnesia Plot: How 1940s films reinvented the ways stories are told onscreen' (*Lapham's Quarterly*, 2017).

This chapter also develops the concept of *bildungsroman*, which is one of the persistent themes in this book. There is a strong scholarship around this concept within literary studies, and I have been influenced by the work of Mikhail Bakhtin, particularly his essay 'The Bildungsroman and its Significance in the History of Realism' in *Speech Genres and Other Late Essays* (University of Texas Press, 1996) and Franco Moretti's book *The Way of the World: The*

Bildungsroman in European Culture (Verso, 1987). *Bildungsroman* remains an active area of interest in literary studies and there is a useful special issue of the journal *Textual Practice* (vol. 34, no. 12, 2020) devoted to 'The Bildungsroman: Form and Transformations', edited by John Frow, Melissa Hardie and Vanessa Smith.

When I talk about the 'primal screen' in my discussion of Arabella's inability to remember her trauma, I am invoking the concept of repression as it is theorised within psychoanalysis. The concept of a 'primal screen' is a dual allusion to Freud's essay 'Screen Memories' (1899) and to the later Freudian idea of the 'primal scene', which he most famously articulates in the 'Wolf Man' case study that was published as 'From the History of an Infantile Neurosis' (1918). On the role that trauma plays in returned soldiers, I found Renata Salecl's book *On Anxiety* (Routledge, 2004) very helpful. With respect to paranoia, I am taking my approach from Lacanian psychoanalysis, and a good introduction to this challenging field is the book *Lacan on Psychosis: From Theory to Praxis* (Routledge, 2019), edited by Jon Mills and David Downing, particularly Mills' essay 'Lacan on Paranoiac Knowledge'.

Also introduced in this chapter is the genre known as *film noir,* which refers to crime films that emerged in the Hollywood cinema of the classical period (1930s to 1950s). There is a very considerable literature on *film noir,* but the collection *Shades of Noir* (Verso, 1993), edited by Joan Copjec, is one that I have found particularly useful in theorising the dynamics of this genre. I have also been influenced by Slavoj Žižek's analysis of *noir* in his book *Enjoy Your Symptom!: Jacques Lacan in Hollywood and Out* (Routledge, 2001).

Chapter Three: Repetition

The philosophical heritage of repetition can be traced to Søren Kierkegaard's book *Repetition* (1843), but also runs through Friedrich Nietzsche, Jacques Derrida and Gilles Deleuze. The approach that I take to the concept of repetition is drawn from psychoanalysis, which takes seriously the compulsion we have to repeat actions, circumstances and scenes. While in the case of pleasurable activities this makes sense, it is harder to fathom why we do this with painful things. Freud addressed this in his famous essay 'Beyond the Pleasure Principle' (1920), which was influenced by the treatment of traumatised soldiers serving in the First World War. The concept of repetition was nominated by Jacques Lacan as one of the four 'fundamental' concepts of psychoanalysis in *Book XI* of his *Seminar* series (Norton, 1998).

What I have tried to do in this chapter is to show how repetition is given shape by a desire to know. This desire to know runs up against the repression of trauma; that is, against a countervailing prohibition on knowledge. Repetition is the result of these duelling impulses. As the shows discussed in this chapter demonstrate, repetition erodes the meaning of action, and in this way, each of these texts revolves around reinstating the efficacy of action. Once again, Slavoj Žižek is very insightful on this concept, and I can recommend the chapters 'Why is Suicide the Only Successful Act?' and 'Why is Every Act a Repetition?' from *Enjoy Your Symptom!*

I touch briefly on the idea of the 'metaphysical' detective, since this is a role that Nadia finds herself playing. This concept was introduced in a famous essay by Michael Holquist (one of the founding texts of literary postmodernism) in *New Literary History* titled 'Whodunit and Other Questions: Metaphysical Detective Stories in Post-war Fiction' (vol. 3, no. 1, 1971: 135–56). A recent work in this vein is Antoine Dechêne's *Detective Fiction and the Problem of Knowledge: Perspectives on the Metacognitive Mystery Tale* (Springer, 2018). On the more general issue of why time (as it is conventionally understood) is failing in stories that involve time loops, I highly recommend Todd McGowan's lucid exposition of cinematic time in *Out of Time: Desire in Atemporal Cinema* (University of Minnesota Press, 2011).

Chapter Four: Dissociation

This chapter begins with a consideration of the idea of the 'double' or *doppelgänger*. The first to seriously study this as a literary phenomenon was Otto Rank, in his book *Der Doppelgänger* in 1914. Rank was a follower of Freud's and this is one of the earliest works of psychoanalytic literary criticism. Other well-known studies include Car Keppler's *The Literature of the Second Self* (University of Arizona Press, 1972) and Karl Miller's *Doubles: Studies in Literary History* (Oxford University Press, 1985).

I also introduce the idea of 'alienated labour' in this chapter, which the show *Severance* throws into relief. The film scholar Mark Bould is useful in thinking about labour as it ge ts represented in science fiction. The final section of his book *Science Fiction* (Routledge, 2012) gives useful examples of the way that globaised labour gets pictured in dystopian films. For a more sustained consideration of the public–private split that capitalism institutes, I can recommend Todd McGowan's book *Capitalism and Desire: The Psychic Cost of Free Markets* (Columbia University Press, 2016), particularly the chapter on 'The Psychic Constitution of Private Space'. Another excellent, but more densely theorised account of these issues is Samo Tomšič's book *The Capitalist Unconscious: Marx and Lacan* (Verso, 2015), and a good starting point is the section on 'The labour theory of the unconscious' in part two of that book.

In this chapter, I speak of the fate of the innies in *Severance*, who know they have someone who acts in the world outside but have no idea what they do, as one of 'castration'. This is a term that generates some understandable alarm and confusion. It refers to the removal of the male genitalia, which is not a common practice in modern societies. One of the controversial claims of psychoanalysis is that the image of this experience lives in fantasy even as it does not take place in reality. The evidence for this surprising assertion is the repeated occurrence of this image in dreams, turns of phrase, word associations and cultural tropes. It is as though this horrific image of 'severance' somehow sits behind every attempt to know ourselves (irrespective of our gender) or to affect the world.

The innies in *Severance* are, in effect, identical to the amnesiacs we saw in *Homecoming*. To say that they have forgotten something (that is, the entirety of their lives) does not quite capture the experience. One is forced to say that they have been shorn of something vital. The representation of those stripped of their memories in both shows – the soldiers in *Homecoming* and the innies in *Severance* – is quite precise. They have been neutered. Good, clear discussions of the psychic phenomenon of castration can be found in Todd McGowan's chapter 'The Signification of the Phallus' in the collection *Reading Lacan's Écrits* (Routledge, 2018). The final section of Alenka Zupančič's book *The Odd One*

In: On Comedy (MIT Press; 2008), which is amusingly titled '(Essential) Appendix: The Phallus', is also quite helpful in situating the idea of castration as pivotal to sexual difference.

The other term that arises in this chapter (and elsewhere in the book) is 'dramatic irony'. In literary criticism, dramatic irony occurs when the reader (in poetry or prose) or audience (in drama) knows something that a character does not. In staged dramas, for instance, something can be happening in view of the audience but out of view of certain characters. Children at pantomimes enjoy the game of dramatic irony. As the villain or monster looms silently behind the hero, they cry out: 'Behind you! He's behind you!' They delight as the hero spins around only for the villain to adroitly disappear. Dramatic irony is thus a game that formalises the structure of knowledge as something consisting of what is known to be known and known to be unknown. A lot of the suspense and humour of narratives would collapse without dramatic irony. This is also the structure of the unconscious.

Conclusion: The upside down

This conclusion mainly recapitulates ideas introduced earlier in the book, but it does make reference to the proposition that television is traditionally understood as having a 'pedagogical' role. This idea goes back to the early theorisation of television by the British New Left, where television was conceived as having a role in civic education. Raymond Williams' book *Television: Technology and Cultural Form* (Harper Collins, 1974) was a notable early formulation of this stance.

In many ways, television (and broadcast culture more generally, including radio and cinematic newsreels) was a successor to print culture. The emergence of a 'public sphere' was essential to the emergence of bourgeois culture as it gave this emergent class its political validity as the expression of public will. This argument has famously been made by Jürgen Habermas, particularly in his essay 'The Public Sphere: An Encyclopedia Article' published in *New German Critique* (no. 3, 1974: 49–55), and was also at the heart of Benedict Anderson's hugely influential book *Imagined Communities: Reflections on the Origin and Spread of Nationalism* (Verso, 1983).

The centrality of media to modern public life has resulted in the expression 'print capitalism', which draws from Anderson's work. Much contemporary work in media studies considers these kinds of issues. The emergence of new media has dramatically changed the public sphere (in many ways the internet and social media obliterate the lines between public and private) with major domestic and geopolitical repercussions. A prescient account of these issues can be found in Tauel Harper's *Democracy in the Age of New Media: The Politics of the Spectacle* (Peter Lang, 2011). In terms of television, John Hartley's book on *The Uses of Television* (Routledge, 2002) emphasises the role that television continues to have in educating its citizenry. The programming of broadcast television contains numerous shows aimed at teaching you to cook, garden, renovate, travel, fish, dance and so on. John Hartley's essay 'Television as Transmodern Teaching' is also helpful and can be found in *Television: The Critical View* (Oxford University Press, 2006), edited by Horace Newcomb.

Acknowledgements

Nothing tempers an idea like a sceptical student. So, my first debt is to those students who have come to my lectures over the years in 'Narrative in the Digital Age' and 'Netflicks: Cinema and Long-form Television' at the University of Western Australia, armed with their curiosity and scepticism. The field of contemporary television is fast-moving and my students have been faithful allies in tracking its movements and modulations. I am proud to say that *Netflicks: Conceptual Television in the Streaming Era* was forged in the crucible of the classroom.

I owe a special debt of gratitude to the friends that read this book in draft form and offered frank and insightful advice. Thank you, Sarah Collins, Tauel Harper and Laurent Shervington. I would also like to thank Ned Curthoys, Ann Curthoys, Ethan Blue, Cameron Muir, Daniel Juckes and Tanya Dalziell for reading an early portion of this book and providing crucial guidance and practical suggestions. I would particularly like to acknowledge Ned Curthoys for awakening my interest in the *bildungsroman*, a concept that plays a significant role in this book.

UWA Publishing have been wonderful in developing this new Vignettes series and allowing my book to open it. In particular, I am grateful to Kate Pickard, Jill Benn and the UWAP Board for their support. Time will tell whether their faith was justified. A special thank you to Melanie Dankel for her expert editing of the manuscript.

The book has been enhanced by a number of stills from the shows that I discuss. I would like to acknowledge and thank the rights holders for allowing these stills to be published in illustration of my arguments. Thank you to Lauren Pratt for her work on sourcing these stills and the permission to use them.

Finally, I would like to thank Wai Sum Woo and Joseph Hughes-d'Aeth for their love and support. I wrote this book while on long-service leave, which many would think insane, but for me was a pleasure and a privilege. Yet, without Wai Sum and Joseph, I would probably have been lost.